PUNCH ME IN THE FACE

RESILIENCE TRAINING THAT WILL GUARANTEE YOU SUCCESS

BY SHAWN MEAIKE

PUNCH ME IN THE FACE
Copyright © 2023 by 2 Market Media

All rights reserved. No portion of this book may be reproduced, stored in a retrieval system, or transmitted in any form or by any means - electronic, mechanical, photocopy, recording, scanning, or other - except for brief quotations in critical reviews or articles, without the prior written permission of the publisher.

Published by 2 Market Media with Punch Media, LLC.

ISBN 979-8-218-14349-7 (PB)

Printed in the USA by 48 Hour Books (www.48HrBooks.com)

TABLE OF CONTENTS

Foreword 5
Chapter 1: Why Do I Need To Be Punched In The Face? 7
Chapter 2: Will Can Be Taught—You Are Not Just Born With It
.... 19
Chapter 3: It Is Not Talent Nor Brains That Breeds Success ... 29
Chapter 4: Finding Your North Star 39
Chapter 5: Creating Daily Habits 49
Chapter 6: Remove All Negative Influences 55
Chapter 7: Bury Your Sh*t In A Box 59
Chapter 8: Setting Big Goals 65
Chapter 9: Punch In The Face Training 75
Chapter 10: Never Worry About What Other People Think ... 85
Chapter 11: Never Take A Step Backwards—No Retreat 99
Chapter 12: Live By The Standards: "I Am Humble, I Have No
Fear And Every Day Is Great" 109
Chapter 13: Stand Up For Others Who Can't Stand Up For
Themselves 115
Chapter 14: Time To Move Fast 123
Chapter 15: How Do You Want To Be Remembered? 129
About the Author 137

FOREWORD

Shawn Meaike is truly a man of the people. Occasionally in life, you meet someone who has not only achieved remarkable success, but teaches you how to leave no one behind along the journey.

I remember the day that Shawn walked into my life. I am the CEO of a charity that houses seven hundred people a day in an old remodeled hospital called the Dream Center. Shawn was on a tour of our campus with other influential leaders to see the ways we are attacking issues of homelessness and addiction. The business leaders considered it, "A fact-finding mission." Shawn saw the tour as an opportunity to make a difference. The bus loaded up at the end of the tour and the business leaders headed back to their hotel, moved by what they experienced after hearing various stories of wayward lives trying to find their way home. However, Shawn was not only moved by what he saw, he was stirred to action. He called me on the phone and boldly proclaimed in his unique leadership style that he would spend his life serving the poor and afflicted.

From that day on, it became an endless passion for Shawn to visit the homeless, addicted, and afflicted that reside in our building and coach them back to life. He looked people in the eye with compassion and spoke to every individual with a spark that I've never seen in three decades of outreach ministry. Our residents were taken aback by this successful man spending his valuable time speaking to them like they were the most important people in the world. Shawn not only spoke to their needs, but to their potential.

The success story of Shawn's business, Family First Life, isn't confined to just business principles and effective strategies—it's based on the foundation that love is the most powerful force in the world. It's an army of agents that live each day of their lives consumed with a desire to find a need and fill it, find a hurt and heal it. Everything about Shawn's leadership style is direct and honest, but more than that, rooted in belief beyond the surface clichés that people can succeed.

Punch Me in the Face will teach you so much about the reality of leadership. This book is going to take you on a wild ride of relatable experiences that few will dare to explore. A great leader will take you on the journey and allow you to see the setbacks, the wins, and the glorious times when getting back up carries the foundation of their success. This book will cause you to laugh, cry, and give you the gift of resiliency that is desperately needed in our world today. Thank you, Shawn, for writing this book. Get ready because these pages contain real and honest leadership principles that come straight from the heart of a man who truly is a fan of life and a fan of others who leaves no one behind.

Matthew Barnett
Founder, LA Dream Center

1.

WHY DO I NEED TO BE PUNCHED IN THE FACE?

Punches are Inevitable. Learn From Them.

The first time I was punched in the face, I was probably seven or eight. My bus stop had this teenage idiot who would pick fights with the younger kids. One day, this teenager was making fun of my friend's jean jacket because it was dirty. None of us had a lot of money. I got in front of him to tell him to knock it off and he punched me in the face. My eyes watered up. I was stunned; yes, that he actually punched me, but more so that I didn't die. That was a big deal because I had just taken this huge hit but realized I was actually ok. I just stood there. I was still just a little kid and wasn't going to win in a fight with a teenager, but I still felt powerful because I knew I could take it.

Later, I recalled this moment as an underclassman in high school and finally playing football. I can remember the very first kickoff of the very first game on a Friday night and seeing how big the crowd was to me. During the kickoff, you were either a laneman, where you had a lane assigned to you, or you were a headhunter. I was a headhunter, so I ran directly to where the ball was. But—if I missed a tackle—it was a massive missed opportunity. It was me not doing my job and I didn't want to screw that up. The crowd was so excited and cheering and I just remember running down the field thinking that I didn't want to screw this up in front of all of these people. And then I got leveled. I was completely blindsided and I didn't see it. As I got up, I was a little bit dizzy and had snot running down my nose as I was looking for my mouthpiece. It was then I realized that 1. The entire crowd wasn't staring at me, they weren't focused only on what I was doing. 2. As it was with the bully, I was fine. I didn't die. I could take it. I could do this. Life was good.

I learned that I could take a hit. I learned how to get punched in the face. I also learned that you just have to give it everything you got and do the best you can to win. You think everybody in the world's focused on everything you're doing, but they're not. It was a big deal, going from playing in front of some parents to playing for thousands. I knew I might fail, but I still had to try, even if it meant getting punched in the face. The reason you have to get punched in the face is that you have to know that you're going to survive.

Now, literally getting punched in the face teaches you that lesson really quickly. But other metaphorical kinds of punches in the face have plenty to teach you too. If you're going to progress in anything in life and live the life you want, there are going to be some punches along the way. No one ever got to where they are without some setbacks. Whether you're an entrepreneur, athlete, or parent, everyone gets punched in the face sooner or later. You have to on your road to success. But you can take it—if you really want it.

Why Aren't You Getting Punched?

A lot of people spend their lives avoiding being punched in the face. It's why the road to success is the road less traveled. People would rather have boring, cushy, poor-paying jobs than take the risk of getting punched in the face.

At the end of the day, especially in business, you have to make decisions like you're down to your last thousand dollars. You have to ask yourself, is this decision going to actually lead you somewhere? Because being broke can feel like getting punched in the face. You have to decide if you're going to get back up and try again, or fail and live with the feeling that a punch knocked you down for good.

I remember getting my life insurance license and needing to buy some leads. Leads are the lifeblood of basically anyone in commission-based sales. I had kids to feed, but I spent my last thousand bucks on leads thinking it would pay off. Nope, I made zero sales. I got punched in the face. But I wasn't afraid to invest in myself, so I broke out my credit card—despite the 23% interest rate—and tapped into it. I thought, let me try again and buy more.

Boom—punched in the face again. No sales, no money. I learned from those mistakes, bought more leads, and finally made some sales. Striking out and making no sales is just another punch in the face and another obstacle that is to be expected in any sales position. You can't let the punch affect you because they are inevitable. You must get yourself back up and try again.

When I got into real estate, I interviewed a company called Remax and they had two commission plans. One was 95%—which is good—with a desk fee of $2,000 a month, or it was 55% with no desk fee. I chose the high comp (95%) because I realized that even though I had to pay the desk fee, the higher comp still provided a MUCH better opportunity to make money. Working for double the commission is ultimately the better choice, even if it means taking the initial punch.

I wasn't trying to hedge my bets. I just wanted to give it everything I got. I really believed in myself, so when I looked at being out that $2,000 and getting punched in the face, I went for it—even though it might have taken me longer to make a profit. Let's say I sold a house at $150,000 and got 3% of it. That would be $4,500—unless I represented both the buyer and the seller. If I did the 55%, I made $2,475. Now, if I took the 95% commission, I got $4,275. Since I'd probably sell 12 to 14 houses a month, that paid for my monthly desk fee and then some.

I couldn't comprehend why people took the lower comp. Everyone that chose the 55% didn't believe in themselves; they didn't want to get punched in the face. And in the end, I made more money over time. I believed in myself enough to get hit and reap the rewards later.

A lot of people avoid getting punched in the face but almost everybody you meet in business that is successful and self-made will tell you the story of when they spent every dollar they had, when they made the ultimate sacrifice, when they were terrified and got themselves punched in the face and got right back up.

The Other Side of the Punch

The beauty of this is that anyone can get back up, but a lot of people don't.

During my first week of varsity baseball, we were introduced to pitching machines. One of the first drills we did was to get into the batting cage and set the pitching machine up at 80 mph. They would put 10 balls in there and you had to learn to take a hit; you'd turn and get hit in the ass or the leg. There were people that didn't want to do that, or simply wouldn't. But the objective is to get on base, and if I can get a free base because you hit me with a ball and I'm not going to die, then I meet that objective.

You have to decide: Are you willing to take a hit? Because fearlessness doesn't come from being some big tough guy. Fearlessness comes from understanding that the consequences don't outweigh the reward—the reward outweighs the consequence. The reward of getting hit by a pitch is to be accepted and relevant, for people to cheer for me, for my teammates to like me, for the other people at school to like me, and to feel accomplished. While the hit is going to hurt instantaneously when the ball makes contact, what hurts a lot more is losing out on all those rewards, which is a consequence in and of itself.

In sports, business, and in life, the only way you learn is by getting hit. That's what teaches you to be fearless. Get hit once and you can get hit 1,000 times. It doesn't matter. What matters is that the first time you get hit by a pitch, or dragged five yards by a bigger player because the next time someone tries dragging you five yards before the tackle, you will have learned how to take them down sooner.

I used to coach youth football and the first thing we did is find out which kids were afraid. The other coaches thought you couldn't teach them not to be afraid. I called bullsh*t. You can't teach kids to be more athletic, but you can teach them to keep their heads up and make contact. Now, if the kid isn't willing to try or hates it and isn't willing to keep doing it, that's a possibility. But some will take the hit and can deal with it.

Maybe you're reading this and thinking how you're getting punched in the face because your job should pay more. I was a social worker for 14 years and didn't make anything. I got punched in the face on a daily basis. As a child protective service worker, I only got involved in a family's life if there was a report of abuse and/or neglect—if a child under the age of 18 was abandoned or being harmed physically, sexually, or emotionally. I only showed up if there was an extremely valid reason, yet I still had people cuss me out and yell at me.

At this job, I was a training supervisor for years and the first thing I taught the trainees was that you can't have fear. People aren't literally going to punch you in the face for the most part, but figuratively, they're going to want to punch you in the face. They're going to say derogatory things to you, make fun of you, try to get under your skin, and make you afraid. But you have to be willing to deal with that because there is a child's safety at risk. It's why you need to always keep in mind what matters, or what I call your north star (more on this later). As a social worker, I knew the consequence was severe and that kids could get hurt, so the reward for me was protecting them. Sure, the parents would yell at me and try to intimidate me and that might make me uncomfortable, but there was a bigger problem if I let them manipulate me. Once you're unshakeable, you're really hard to deal with.

What to Do When You Get Hit

When you get hit, it's up to you to decide what you're going to do. When it happens, whether it's in business or in life, you're going to get this weird feeling in your stomach and have to decide what's going to happen next.

I decided to go skydiving and—to be honest—when I went up in this tiny little plane and looked out, I didn't want to jump. But I was with all these other people and thought, there's no way I'm going to avoid getting punched in the face and not be the only person that doesn't jump and has to go back down in the airplane. I knew it would be scary for a minute, but I knew I couldn't live with myself if I didn't jump. That would be the bigger punch.

You're going to have to make those decisions in life and business. I tell people the only way they're going to grow in sales is by getting punched in the face. If you're not good at it, you have to push harder.

People will tell me they're pushing as hard as they can to make a sale, and I'll say, "Ok, why don't you push hard enough where you think they're actually going to ask you to leave the house?" If you've never been asked to leave the house, you're not pushing hard enough. You're not getting uncomfortable enough.

Nothing good happens until people are uncomfortable. But a lot of us are conditioned to run around and try to stay comfortable. I'm not saying go out and pick fights with people for no reason. You should want to be the bigger person and take the high road. But sometimes you have to go ahead, square up, and get ready to fight. There's a time to square up and punch life in the face. But you have to ask yourself on a daily basis: Where am I getting punched in the face and where am I making decisions in life to avoid that?

There is going to be conflict in your relationships and discussions. Any decision that's a good decision was probably a hard decision. Maybe you had to make a decision leaving one person happy and another person upset. Hard decisions usually lead to something great. Easy decisions are just decisions you make on a daily basis, like what am I going to eat? What about asking yourself if you're drinking too much? That's hard. Should I stop? Even harder.

You have to ask yourself all these things as you're moving through life. When I decided to quit drinking and using drugs, I got punched in the face. When I decided to quit, I had to renegotiate every relationship in my life. My friends were all people who partied hard. They weren't bad people, I just knew I wasn't going to be doing the things they were doing anymore. I couldn't. I knew it was going to affect my relationships. Most people think when you're in a relationship and you get sober, that it's a good thing for the relationship. But when you have a problem, you tend to be in an enabling relationship where your addiction feeds something for them. So when you get healthy and take that away, it can really screw up your relationship. It sounds wacky, but it's true. It definitely negatively impacted the relationships I had at that time, which I didn't see coming. So I got punched in the face every night. I couldn't sleep for about a year. I didn't decide I was going to start drinking again to stop the punching, I just took it. Sometimes you have to take the beating to get to the other side.

If you really want to change, then you have no choice but to change. If you hate your job, if it's not providing enough for your family, if your boss never gives you time off, if you don't like how the company treats you, and it's a dead end, then sooner or later, going out and doing your own thing and taking that punch won't hurt nearly as bad as staying in that dead-end job.

We can't avoid getting punched in the face if we're going to move forward. When I launched the insurance company I work at, people said I was going to get sued by my previous insurance company. I knew it was going to be a risk, but I had to move forward. When I quit, they asked what I was going to do and I said, "life insurance." They said I couldn't. Technically, we had a non-compete in place, which is very standard in the insurance world; however, to me, it made no sense to be a "captive" agent. I could get leads anywhere. I could get trained anywhere. I could get carrier contracts anywhere. All the things they provided me, I could have gotten in multiple places. Nevertheless, the non-compete was for two years and they said they could sue me.

I said, "Listen, here's the way it's going to work. I'm going to go sell life insurance because I have a life insurance license. I'm independent. I'm not beholden to you. But I'm letting you know, if you sue me, then I'm going to recruit every single person I can recruit from the company. I want you to know that."

A lot of people came with me of their own volition and I was still sued. They got a restraining order against me and said I couldn't run my company anymore. I talked to my lawyers and I didn't think I was in violation of the contract because I didn't solicit anyone to come work with me.

I said to my lawyers, "Listen, I don't care if they're working with me or not, I'm going to keep working. They're going to think it's a violation, but let's have the court figure it out. In the meantime, I'm going to keep moving forward."

I wasn't afraid of taking those punches. I was just going to get back up and keep moving forward. That other company did everything it could to put me out of business because they didn't want to compete with me. Needless to say, I survived and my company has since grown immensely.

Punch Your Way Through Regret
Everybody wants to stand up for the right thing. Everybody wants to stand up for the person being bullied, but a large majority of people don't because they don't want to be punched in the face, and then they live with regret.

Early on in my life, I never thought I was the ultimate fighting champion. I was good at fighting because I wasn't afraid, but I was by no means a black belt. I was never afraid to get hit because I knew the result—it wasn't going to be that bad. I knew the consequence of running through my life and avoiding being punched in the face was going to be much worse.

I never want people to think I'm scared. There are people better than me, bigger than me, stronger than me, but no one can take a hit like I can. I can take a punch and I'll keep rolling. I had a very difficult childhood and made horrible adolescent decisions, but I look at them as blessings now. I started drinking when I was 10. I started using drugs when I was 12. The first time I got arrested I was 14—and I got arrested eight more times from the age of 14 to the age of 23. But again, I wouldn't change any of it. I learned from all of those uncomfortable situations. I learned early on in life from my father's side of the family that you had to stand up for yourself and stand your ground—always. And while my parents split up when I was young—and I didn't see my father nearly as much as I saw my mother—it helped me become the man that I am today. I wouldn't trade any of my experience, because I've learned from them all. God is in charge. I'm just walking in his steps.

I'm not saying getting punched doesn't suck. It just doesn't have to be so bad, especially because the alternative it worse. And it does get easier.

Let's say you decide you want to get up earlier to work out. The first time you get up at 5:00 AM, it will suck. It will feel like a punch. But you know what? At some point in time, you have to make a decision on what matters to you. And when you go back to that, the punches don't feel so hard.

The other thing that happens when you start taking punches is it actually attracts people to you. They see you're not afraid. It's like the bully that wants to befriend you once you take the punch. It's over and people actually respect you more.

Think about all the successful people in this world. You look at their stories and the number of times they were punched in the face and just kept getting back up. Getting punched in the face is part of the process. If you want to be successful and move forward, you cannot avoid it.

Go for getting punched in the face today. If you've been trying to get the sale, show up and don't leave until you get it. If you've been waiting to ask for a promotion, a new job title, or a new job assignment but you've been too scared of getting punched in the face, now's your chance. When you're in a room full of people and you have a question but are too scared of looking stupid, raise your hand. If you're scared of letting your kids try something new, take the punch anyway to help them grow.

Be vulnerable as hell and allow yourself to get punched. Because every time that happens and you survive, people will start paying attention to you. Start looking to get punched in the face, not avoiding it. I know it's not easy, which is why if you keep reading, I'll help you get through it. And I promise, everything in your life will change.

2.
WILL CAN BE TAUGHT—YOU ARE NOT JUST BORN WITH IT

Where There's a Will…

People often comment on how I must've been born with a really strong will. It's because whenever I say I'm going to do something, I always, always do it. But I wasn't born with it—I developed it. And the truth is, anyone can. But how?

First of all, you start to develop the right structure to set you up for success. You do that by creating short-term goals, which give you a sense of urgency. Set a lofty goal: A goal that would be amazing to hit, but also knowing that it could not necessarily be unattainable because it's extremely difficult to hit. A goal where you need to bring your A-game, day in and day out. Then set short-term goals to reach it.

Since bringing your A-game every day is difficult in of itself, you need to have a fallback goal, or a drop-dead goal. For example, if your goal is to make $1M dollars in sales, knowing that if you hit it you gave your absolute best effort every day, then you need to understand that you cannot be mad at yourself or feel like a failure if you only sell $750k. Especially if it's progress from the previous year, $750k should still be considered an accomplishment.

Let's say you want to go from not working out at all to working out five days a week. Then you would go for it and your drop-dead goal would be that you can't miss three for the first month. Write your daily goals out every day and cross them out when they're done, which is another way to help ensure you do it.

If you wanted to get good at kickboxing, you'd set up time to kick a lot. But you'd also develop tough shins by getting kicked a lot. After a while, you won't even feel it anymore. When I took my kids to karate and I got them in kickboxing classes, we started kicking things like poles without any shin guards on so that it would numb their shins after a while. "Will" is having the understanding that there are two sides to each coin. Getting good at kickboxing doesn't only mean getting good at kicking. You have to understand that you will also be kicked a lot and taking a kick is just as important to becoming a good kickboxer.

You need to live a life where you make your decisions based on what you have to do today. Will is doing what you have to do on a regular basis, not what you want to do. Start small to develop your will.

I got a sauna and started thinking about how long I could stay in it. I looked up the world record and I read the record holder died, so that was kind of over the top. He had his at 200 degrees and mine only went to 170. But I still wondered how long I could stay in. I went in my first day and thought, I'll do this for 30 minutes. Well, I lasted eight minutes. But I told myself, tomorrow, I'll do 10.

I did 10 for a few days, then 15 minutes for a week, 17 for another week… I developed my will to stay longer and longer and eventually got to those 30 minutes. It was hard but not as hard as trying to do it right away. I needed to develop the will to stay in longer.

Developing will is about accomplishing things in bite-size chunks. And it's also about doing it every day. That can be for anything you decide you want to do.

When I wanted to stop drinking and using drugs, I actually still drank. I thought, what if, for the first 30 days, my bite-sized chunk was that I stopped drinking on Tuesdays? I used to drink seven days a week, but I thought I could make a point to NOT drink on Tuesday to start. I just picked one day out of the week and that was it. For the first 30 days, I didn't drink on Tuesdays but did drink on the other six days of the week. Then I progressed to Tuesdays and Wednesdays. Because not drinking on the weekend wasn't an option for me at that point (I knew I would fail) and Monday and Thursday nights were for football. But Tuesday and Wednesday basically had nothing going on (no social gatherings to drink at), so they were the easiest and attainable to focus on as a short-term goal.

Let's take your job. Maybe you're starting to realize you need to develop a will for the grind. Start by setting some bite-sized goals.

My first job right out of college was for the state of Connecticut. I asked what the minimum time would be that it would take to get promoted. I was told I had to be there for more than one year to apply to become a supervisor. So at that year mark, I applied to be a supervisor—and I didn't get it. I was interviewing alongside people who had been there 10, 20, 30 years. So, I learned how to interview. But I was also fearless, had backbone, and had a will. I interviewed another time and another.

The third time, I got the job. The first thing I asked was: How do you get promoted to program supervisor? I was told I would need a master's degree. I thought, damn, I don't have one of those. They said they'd pay for it. So I went to school for nights and weekends while I still had my job and got my master's degree in a year and a half. And I applied for the program supervisor position. But they said I needed a minimum of five years. I only had two. But I thought, who determined that rule? I went for it anyway and got the job.

That was the start of my grit. I was always trying to figure out how I get more and how I could challenge myself to be better.

When I got into real estate, I didn't have any money. I didn't go to my family because they didn't have any money either. I went to the people that have the most money—banks. I applied for a construction loan for a sizable amount and was told no. I went to another big bank and was told no. I went to a local bank and asked if I could meet with the president of the bank and was told no and they handed me to a VP. I convinced this VP to let me meet with this president because it was about an investment in a project he wasn't going to want to miss out on. I told them I had a wealth of experience in real estate, even though I was 26 and brand new to construction. But I managed to convince him to let me meet with the president.

I will never forget that meeting. His name was James and he let me come into his office and asked how he could help. I said I had been a real estate agent for years now and I was getting into construction and subdivisions. I laid out my whole plan, my excitement, what I was going to do, who I was, what I was all about.

He asked, "How much money do you think you would need?"

I said, "Well, I can buy a lot for 40 grand and the construction for $160k. All in, 200K and I'll sell for 320K."

I didn't have much leverage, only a small house. So even though it was very unconventional, he said, "I'll do it, but you have to pay us back in six months. You'll start making payments immediately when you draw all the money, and the loan balloons up in six months."

I agreed and we shook hands. And I did it—I paid him back within six months.

I went back to him for my next project, only this time, I needed a million dollars.

Again, he said, "If you get this done in six months, I will give it to you."

I think he thought I wouldn't do it, but I got the house done, sold, and closed in four and a half months.

I kept developing. I was always looking to put myself in a position where I was going to do more and more, developing myself like I was developing calluses.

You'll have a hard time at first, but once you keep building, keep developing those calluses, you'll be able to do more and more. I've had calluses for 30 years. They're not going anywhere because I work on them every day and they were developed on sheer will.

What Can You Do and What Are You Willing to Do?
You need to be realistic about what's possible. A lot of people want to talk about things they can't achieve because they don't want to be held accountable. You're not going to grow or develop that way. People want their life to be like a movie, but life is not a movie. I wish I had a nickel for everybody I knew who watched *Goodfellas* and thought they were a gangster and got their ass kicked. When you live in a fantasy world, you're not developing a will. You've got your head in the clouds instead of planting your feet on the ground and working on your goals.

What are you actually doing? What are you willing to do?

Five-year plans are for losers. Five-year plans don't have you looking at what you're doing today. You can't get ahead if you have some arbitrary five-year plan. What are you doing TODAY?

Actually, I think about what I want to do the least today and I do that first to get it out of the way. Otherwise, you'll just keep avoiding it. You have to change today and work on what you need to do today.

You also need to redefine the nature of your association. Look at the people you're hanging out with. Look at the people that you listen to, that you watch on TV, that you read. Redefine the nature of all your relationships and the association you have because you are who you associate with.

I took two weeks off from the sauna and when I came back, I could only do 22 minutes. I told myself it was ok, but it was not. The minute you backtrack, you're in trouble. If you're not moving forward, your will weakens.

You can't back down. You develop will when you choose not to back down. You can only do that if you don't have a fear of failure or judgment. You can't develop will by worrying about whatever's going to happen or what people are going to think. I could have never convinced that bank to give me that loan if I was scared about what they were going to do or say. I could have never gotten a promotion with the state if I cared about what others thought.

You have to tune that stuff out to develop a will. Get uncomfortable. Build the resistance to not be afraid or intimidated by anybody in any way, shape, or form. Don't care about where you did or didn't go to school. Don't worry about what people say.

Your Childhood Has Nothing to Do With It

People think I have will because my mom worked three jobs and my dad was hardly around, so I have will because of how I was raised. Bullsh*t. I have this will because I chose to develop it throughout my adult life. I have this will because I decided to work on it every single day. You can have four people grow up in the same house and go on completely different paths. What you decide to do has nothing to do with how you were raised, so stop letting that define you.

You are not born with a will. You create will by watching other people in your life. I emulated others in my life—none of which I am related to—and I watched the will that they had. They had the will to succeed, the will to survive, the will to fight for what was right, the will to challenge, and the will to be uncomfortable. I found people that had all of that so I could learn from and be like them, and I emulated them. I didn't need the perfect family and the perfect childhood to raise me to do that. I know will can be taught because there are people who have it regardless of the kind of upbringing they had.

The world doesn't care how you grew up. You don't get any special discount. You don't get more time to work on your exams or to pay your rent or your mortgage. You still have to pay your taxes at the same time as your boss. The world doesn't care. The world's a pretty harsh place when you look at it because it just keeps moving, with or without you.

You can't control your past, but *you* can keep moving. Some people have gone through some really tough stuff, and I'm sorry for that. I really am. But mostly everyone has gone through some sort of sh*t in their lives. And when you get a handle on that, everything changes.

I had a coach named John for a travel baseball team. He played professional baseball and was a really great guy. I wanted to get to know him.

I said, "Coach, the season's over. Can I get a job with you?"

He could have said no, but instead, he said, "What can you do?"

I said, "Whatever you pay me for."

He said, "Be at this job site tomorrow morning at 7:00 AM."

I said, "I'll be there."

I worked the entire summer for him in property management. I picked his brain, watched all the crews, and watched his properties get transformed. I listened to him talk about real estate, about banking.

My friends thought I was so lucky to get a job from him. But it wasn't luck. I asked, I showed up, I worked the whole day, and I didn't complain. Anybody could have done that. But most people won't. I wasn't born with that kind of will—I had to develop it.

I watched him. I listened to what he said. I watched the way he approached things. He had a fearlessness about him, which I liked. That's why I followed him. I wanted to know what he knew. I wanted to know how he developed it. I wanted to know why he thought he'd win. I wanted to know why a former athlete who didn't really have that experience thought he would be successful in business. He was probably the person that I think had the most will that I'd ever met. And certainly the toughest person I'd met.

The main thing I learned from John was that while he was born with athletic ability that let him play professional baseball for many years, he wasn't born with the will to make it. He developed that over time, or rather, he chose to develop that over time. He chose to participate and he chose to fight.

I was inspired by him. He wasn't born with will and neither was I. But I saw how essential it was to cultivate it for success. I watched the way he carried himself and I wanted to emulate that.

You develop that will by watching, emulating, duplicating, replicating, and then continuing to challenge yourself every day. I tell myself every day I'm going to wake up and find something I can do to test my will, personally or professionally. Those opportunities are everywhere. Maybe you haven't talked to a relative in years. Time to make a phone call. Maybe you're working on patience. There are things you need to be patient about every day, like waiting in line for coffee and not reacting. If you open your eyes and look for them, you'll find them.

If you can do that every single day and you can seek it out, you will develop will. And the best part is, anyone can do it. It's not something you're born with or without. It's something you develop over the course of time—if you choose to.

3.
IT IS NOT TALENT NOR BRAINS THAT BREEDS SUCCESS

You Must Be Relentless

If you were to dissect success, you would see the common denominator isn't brains nor talent but relentlessness. Think about several of the most successful people you know in life and business. Now take that same group and ask yourself: do you believe that they're intellectually smarter than you? Are they the smartest people in the world?

If I think of the five smartest people I've encountered in my life, they're broke as sh*t. Broke as sh*t to me means they have to make decisions in life based on money. Anytime you live your life and you have to make your decisions based on money—whether it's for a kid's college, vacation, retirement, donations, whatever—that means you're broke. Broke as sh*t is when you're borrowing money from people. And the five smartest people I know in the world, IQ-wise, borrow money from people to get by.

So it's not brains that get you to the top. What about talent? Talent beats hard work, and hard work beats talent when talent doesn't work hard. Except when it comes to professional athletics;

then, talent is essential. I don't care how often you swing a bat, you're not going to beat Aaron Judge. Michael Jordan and Kobe Bryant both worked really hard. But even if they didn't really practice, they would still kick the sh*t of almost everybody. They're too talented.

But when it comes to whatever industry you're in, you're not born with that kind of talent. I've met CEOs in charge of massive companies. You think God said, "Hey, Ed Bastian, I gave you the talent to be the CEO of Delta." No. Ed lived his life accumulating information, real-life information, and moved up the ranks. The guy's a hard worker. He's not a positional leader. He's not above things. He has just kicked ass and taken names. God didn't give him or you a business talent.

The ability to make money and be successful business-wise doesn't require talent or intellectual capacity. As a matter of fact, have you heard the phrase, "A+ students work for the C students"? Well, that's a pretty true statement, and I am living proof. I see it all the time in my work. That's because the people that grind, the people that are a little bit crazy and believe they can do anything, are the ones that have been the most successful people that I've been around, but they couldn't care less about their grades in school because they didn't matter. The majority of entrepreneurs I know and have read about in books say they weren't great students in school. I think that the reason I wasn't a great student is I was really focused on getting done with school. Entrepreneurs are independent by nature. We're not C students because we're dumb. It's because we don't give a sh*t.

There's nothing wrong with being the greatest employee in the world. You can do really well and make a lot of money as an employee. But I think a lot of us are busy thinking about what we could do next to go out there and make a living for ourselves. I watched my mom work three jobs and I did not want to do that. I had no problem working hard, but I didn't need to do that to get a grade.

Relentless people are hard workers. That's the common denominator.

It's not that relentless people aren't afraid of anything—they just decide not to be. Relentless people don't take no for an answer. Whatever they touch seems to turn to gold because they relentlessly pursue it. It doesn't take a special talent to do that.

But we'd rather believe it's talent or brains or whatever—something we're not capable of—to keep us safe. Because if we believe that anyone has the capacity to be successful, then that means that YOU are the problem.

I was reading an article the other day about a guy who was intellectually superior to the average person, but his life was in shambles. Why? Because he wasn't relentless. He has poor life habits even though he has a high IQ.

But in the business world, you don't need those talents. As a matter of fact, spend some time talking to successful people and you'll be very appropriately unimpressed. I was so excited to start getting around people that had a lot of money and had been very successful businessmen and women, and I can tell you, they're not any better than me. It was such a relief to see we were similar and there wasn't anything super special about them. Because when you can accept that, that's when your life changes.

Interrogate Your Own Reality

Think about two or three things you haven't achieved in your life. When someone asks you why you haven't been promoted, do you say it's because of something like budget cuts or nepotism? Or can you be honest with yourself that you haven't been relentless enough?

You have to interrogate your own reality. Part of being relentless is being honest with yourself. The minute you're honest with yourself, you have the ability to pursue something relentlessly. Think about two or 20 things in your life that didn't end up the way you wanted them to and be honest about why. I can tell you that everything in my life that didn't end up the way I wanted it to was because of me. There might have been other circumstances and variables, but at the end of the day, I'm still in control of myself. It was my fault.

There's a lot of magic saying, "It's my fault." You want to cleanse your soul to become relentless in order to become successful. The quicker you can learn accountability, and the quicker you can say, "My bad" and mean it, the quicker you'll actually learn and rise to the top. That's easier to learn when you're younger. It's harder if you're starting to do this now, but it's essential.

Me? I'm happy to say I lost my way, drank a little too much, got into some debt, and got lazy. It was my fault. I can work with anybody that says, "It's my fault." To be relentless, there's an accountability factor. Because if everything you're chasing is a facade, then how do you win?

One of the best movies I've ever seen is *Eight Mile*. In the movie, Eminem goes to the rap battle early on and he gets booed off the stage because he chokes. He comes back to the battle later in the movie and starts questioning if he can do it or not. He's got a lot of things pulling against him. He's obviously really poor. He's also in an industry that's not dominated by white people. He's trying to figure out his way in life.

His buddy says, "Aren't you afraid of what they're going to say about you?"

At that moment, he has an epiphany: I know what they're going to say about me, so I'm going to say it first. He gets up there, and basically starts talking about how he's poor, lives with his mom, etc. And he won.

If you do fail and you say it out loud, it's cleansing. There are things you've gone through. What makes me really upset is when successful people only want to talk about their victories. If I want to do what you're doing, and I want to hear your story, and I want to be motivated, I want to know the struggle. That's what's inspiring. Tell me when you had no money in your account, or the litigation you went through, or the disastrous business partner. Walk me through how you got through all of that, because I know it was because you were relentless and wouldn't let up. I want to come out on top too, and I want to know that you went through it so that I know I can get through it too.

It was never ever the talent nor the brains that got you through the struggle—it was your relentless pursuit of what you were looking to achieve. Intellectual capacity and talent are indifferent as it pertains to the struggle. They don't matter, especially when times get tough.

People that are more successful than you are not more talented. It's a hard punch to take because it would be so much easier to blame your lack of success as merely a lack of talent. But once you take it, it's liberating.

A successful guy I wanted to emulate told me, "Shawn, find yourself a great accountant, a great lawyer, and a great financial planner. If you get those three people in your life and they're truly great, that'll allow you to be a guy who grinds and works hard. You don't have to be the smartest one in the room and they can take a lot of that stuff off your plate."

That is advice I'd like to give you because those are the three most important people to put in your life when you're building a business.

Don't let successful people tell you it was their talent or brains that got them there. That's their insecurity pouring out. Because when people start trying to convince you they've had that success because they're great, they're just trying to make sure you don't challenge them in any way, shape, or form. They know that you're probably smarter or more talented than they are. And maybe even more relentless—once given the opportunity.

Put in the Relentless Hours

I'm not really intent on being the most relentless person you've ever met in your life. Relentlessness isn't about being the baddest dude in the building. I never claim to be that guy. What I claim to do, though, is that no matter how much I get hit, I'm always going to get the f@#k up. So if you keep hitting me, you better kill me because I'm never going to stop coming.

That doesn't require talent and it sure as hell doesn't require brains. Sometimes you need to just be dumb enough. For example, when I built my insurance company, I was dumb enough in the beginning to keep very small margins. My margins were tiny, and I didn't make money for years. I used to always joke and say, "Nobody's as dumb as I am."

When I got my insurance license, I worked all day. I went there at 8:00 A.M. and worked until 4:00 P.M. I would leave, get something to eat, and try to sleep for two hours. I had to be at my state job by 10:00 P.M. and worked there until 6:00 A.M. I'd leave there, splash water on my face, and go do it again. I'd work eight to eight Saturday and Sunday. I was dumb enough to do it.

Anytime I meet with somebody trying to become successful and I ask what's holding them back, it's mostly that they aren't putting the hours into it. You also need to focus on your IPAs—your Income Producing Activities. If it doesn't benefit my spiritual life, my family life, my business life, I don't do it.

Take the next 90 days and start watching people who are successful and watch their relentless characteristics and start becoming relentless in your own life. Use them as examples to figure out, where am I relentless? How relentless am I being? Everybody in their life today has an area where they are relentless. You might be relentless about your eating. I'm not trying to be funny, that really might be where you find you're relentless. You can't be relentless in every aspect of your life. I don't want to be relentless at fantasy football or at watching new movies. I don't want to be relentless about my caloric intake either. I want to be smart about what I eat, but I don't want to be relentless about it. I'm just not wired that way.

Whatever those areas are in your life, take the ones that don't benefit you, like drinking too much. That's not funny anymore. Sometimes you have to replace those things with other things to keep you focused. When I stopped drinking and using drugs, I thought I was going to get more focused on becoming a successful businessman. And my business did really well immediately. I started spending time reading and going to meetings. I started attending planning and zoning meetings that weren't even in the towns I lived in just to see who the people were. I started educating myself and getting around mentors. And that's when I started meeting better people and getting around people that knew more than me.

By the way, I recommend you stop drinking. It doesn't really benefit you. Most people can't handle it and they drink their lives away. Even when you only drink a couple of nights a week, it's different now that you're older. You get up later. You feel like crap. Drunk 17-year-olds are funny; drunk 27, 37, 47-year-olds are just pathetic. I'm not judging anybody, I have my own drinking problem. But I can admit it.

The point is, take your relentless behavior and channel it into the positive. Take your natural relentless behavior and bring it somewhere else better.

4.
FINDING YOUR NORTH STAR

You Can't Get Anywhere Without Finding Your North Star

Your north star is your guiding light. It's your compass. The thing you're always focused on. When your world is spinning or crumbling down, what is it you look to? When sh*t hits the fan, there has to be something that leads you. And it can't be 75 different things because there's no way you could be that committed to 75 different things.

When I was in real estate and was a social worker and then was trying to get a couple of other deals, I really had to focus on what was going to make me money. I had to keep my job because I needed benefits, so I kept my state job. And then I decided to transition purely to life insurance in 2008. The other four or five things that paid me a little bit on occasion, I left them alone completely and channeled my energy into this one thing. You can't focus on 10 things to make money, let alone 75. When you have money, you can be an investor and be a passive income earner, but when you don't have the money, you have to be active. You can't be active in that many things.

Early on in my entrepreneurial career, I wanted to provide my children a better life than I ever thought was provided for me. And

I never wanted to say no based on money. That was my humanistic north star. But I also have a spiritual one—my faith—which is important.

When you're working your ass off and the day's awful, and you think there's nothing else you can do, there has to be something that helps guide you. It doesn't have to be a sanctioned religion. The key component of spirituality is that it's a judgment-free zone. I don't judge anybody for being spiritual or not. I don't judge people for agreeing with me or not. I don't judge people at all. But I know when I go lay my head on a pillow at night, I want to know I did right by people, even when it got hard, even when I didn't want to.

You need to have something you believe in that supersedes everything. And if you don't believe in anything outside of yourself, whatever that is, that makes things dangerous.

I'm sitting on the third floor of a sh*tty hotel in Clearwater, Florida after drinking all day long and using drugs. My buddies I play softball with are in the parking lot arguing with another group of guys. I think it's a good idea to jump off the 3rd-floor balcony onto a car below. The car belongs to the guys my buddies were arguing with. So I jump, bounce off the roof of the car, hit my face on the windshield, and cut myself up pretty good. But I'm so drunk and so high, I don't really feel anything. I end up passing out. When I wake up in the morning, I try to get up to go to the bathroom and my sheets are stuck to me because of all the blood.

If you've ever drank that much or got that high and got that numb, you wake up in the morning for a minute and you're thinking, was that a dream or did that really happen? When I saw all the blood, I walked to the bathroom and actually had to peel the sheets off of me. I had gashes all over my face, my legs. But what was harder for me was that I couldn't play in the softball game that day. It was a big tournament and I knew I let my buddies down. Also, the sheriff showed up and they were not happy about all the damage I did.

It was one of the lowest points in my life. In times like these when you're literally and figuratively kicked in the balls, you have two choices: Do I fold or just move on? When you don't have anything bigger guiding you, you'll fold.

Allow those bad times to hurt. Allow it to sink in. Allow the pain to consume you. Not forever, but for that period of time. When it's in there, you'll find your north star to help pull you out.

I'd advise you to find it before then though. You need to do some soul-searching right now. What aligns with your spirituality, your bigger purpose? Again, it's not religion. Believe in something bigger than yourself. You may not even be able to articulate it, nor do you have to. But you need to have something to guide you.

I've truly found my north star. For me, my number one north star is God. Aside from that, it's my kids; they're my responsibility. What overrides everything is God, but on a human level, I take care of my kids. You could even take things to another level and think about everybody in the world. You're supposed to take care of family, employees, coworkers. But you need to find your number one reason for existing on this earth. And you have to ask yourself, what brings you comfort when you're in a really bad place or you're really indecisive, or even when you're really excited?

I'm very spiritual, certainly religious. But I know a lot of very religious people that I don't want to follow anywhere. The Bible tells me not to judge so whatever you believe, I would actually truly not be following my north star if I judged it.

I get nervous when people start to act like God; they freak me out. I can understand why people in today's world are hesitant to talk about God or their beliefs. If you don't believe, I want to listen. And I'll tell you why I believe. I'm all about spreading the word of Christ, but I am not about judging you either because I don't have the right to judge. I'm not God.

And while I don't think you need to believe in God, I do think having a spiritual component is essential. Do you have that in your life? Do you want it? Then you need to go find it.

What Guides You?
People ask how long I'll prepare when I speak to groups, and the answer is... I don't. But then again, I do, meaning I don't in the traditional way, like sitting down and putting pen to paper, bringing notes up, bringing my phone up, etc. Whether I speak for 10 minutes or for four hours to a group, whether there are five people in the group or I've spoken in front of 12,000, I prepare myself regularly by talking to myself. I'm constantly thinking and going through it in my head to have it come out from my heart. I shouldn't have to have notes because I should really be speaking

in my giftedness and I should be speaking in an area that makes perfect sense to me and that I'm passionate about.

I ask people when I hire them, on a scale of one to 10, how much do you like drama, 10 being the highest? Everybody says one because that's the right answer in an interview. When an issue comes up at work, like when Person A tells me Person B isn't doing their job, I'll immediately call Person B in to talk with us. At first, Person A will get flustered and want to backtrack a bit, but I tell them to calm down because if you're telling the truth, there's nothing to be scared of. I only have to do this a couple of times before they'll start talking to each other directly. That's probably one of the biggest distractors from you getting to where you want to go. You need to cut through these distractions by continuously focusing on your north star. I can fix these issues in three minutes instead of letting it be one of a hundred things that lingers for three weeks. If it lingers for three weeks, I can't focus on my north star or anything for that matter.

We can't be afraid to share what guides us, but I don't think we need to scream every minute of every day about it. But I think it's important to share it with the people that work with you, even if they don't agree with you. Where in the world did it say all of us have to agree on things? If you hate me because of my beliefs, my political affiliation, because of what I eat for lunch or what I celebrate, you can respectfully keep that sh*t to yourself; I don't care. I didn't care when I was eight and I don't care now. Instead, I like to be curious and ask questions. In the world of business independent contractor relationships, we need to know something about each other. We need to form relationships. Vulnerability is good. So I ask people:

"Hey man, let me ask you something. You're pursuing this business opportunity and it's going to be a lot of work. What guides you?"

Typically, the answer is going to be family. And that's cool, but I dig deeper: "What do you mean? How many kids? How old are they? Are they all biologically yours?"

"Hey, if you don't mind me asking, is there any spiritual piece behind that?"

Now, I work with all independent contractors so I can ask that but it throws them off. Some people will say their north star is money. I'm not judging, but that will only take you so far.

The successful people I know are the ones where their north star is usually something much bigger and better than making a dollar bill or buying a car and a watch. A lot of times it's spiritual and family. Something's happened to them in their life. There's a cause they believe in, they want to make X amount of dollars to give X amount back. Your north star could be serving people.

It doesn't matter what area you work in. This is how I've always operated since I worked. My very first job at 14 was at the IGA Supermarket in town. At 15, I got my employment papers from the state to work early, and I worked at McDonald's. At 17, I painted the bottoms of boats and also worked at a used car lot. At 18, I got a job at United Parcel Service. I went to the police academy when I was probably 25 or 26. And then transitioned from that to a child protective services worker and did landscaping on the side. I was in real estate and construction in my twenties as well. I built my first house when I was probably 29 and my first subdivision when I was 31. When things weren't going right or even when they were, the Lord has always been my north star. But I also had north stars for the various jobs I was in and businesses I ran.

When I got into real estate, my north star was that I was going to work harder for my clients than anyone else has ever worked for them. When I was in construction, my north star was that I wanted to build the highest quality homes for the fairest price. When I got into life insurance, my north star was that I was going to be the best advocate for my clients. I was going to explain everything to them and be attentive and responsive. When I launched my own life insurance company, my north star was putting the agents and the clients first. Each one of those actually lines up with my ultimate north star, which is God, my faith, just treating people right and fair and good. All those things to me are in alignment. When that north star structure gets out of whack, your life gets out of whack and it makes it hard for people to be productive.

I'm still on a spiritual journey. I have a call in to protect and serve people. I want to help people do better in life. I let all that guide me.

Using Your North Star to Ground You and Guide Others

How do you take your north star and translate it into day-to-day success? The first thing is to use it on a daily basis. On a daily basis, you need to remember why you're doing what you're doing

I read the Bible at night, pray at night, and pray in the morning to get a little time to think about my spirituality and my beliefs privately. My relationship with my kids grounds me.

When I was in real estate, if you didn't pay the rent, I wasn't feeling very Christian. Because I knew if I didn't get the $1,500, it was like they were stealing $750 from each one of my kids. And I didn't want anybody stealing from my kids. That was my guiding north star.

When I launched my life insurance business, I felt like everyone at that time was relying on me. I didn't want to let everybody down. I still had my spiritual and family north stars, but there was that business north star. North stars can be multilevel and multifaceted too in spiritual, family, and business.

The magic is in getting people together who have different north stars. But what is our collective north star, our company's? At my company, our north star is to serve families and to put our clients first. We have to be great. That's not my personal north star but that doesn't matter. If there are 400 people, there might be 190 different north stars. Who cares? Getting everybody to believe and understand and accept people for who they are, what they are, and coming together for the greater good, that's what matters.

Once you can assemble a group of people that have all these different north stars, then you have to figure out what is the north star for your business venture, your opportunity, your company — your mission statement.

If you can identify your ultimate north star, in spirituality, family, and business, and if you can help others identify theirs and teach them that it doesn't matter if they are all different, your life will be in a pretty good place. Then you can teach those people to do it again with their own group of people and you can replicate it and emulate it and then that guiding force allows whatever you're doing to go to the next level.

5.
CREATING DAILY HABITS

The key to being successful is having a healthy self-image. When you have a healthy self-image, it allows you to be much more successful because you're able to accomplish things. When you do that, you feel better. Creating daily habits is so important because it's actually going to be a recipe for success or failure. When you know what to expect of yourself, and you never miss a day, you feel good to accomplish even more.

The two kinds of people I meet are people who are in control of the day or the day controls them. The latter never succeed at a high level. Never.

You need to create daily habits to help you accomplish things. When I started my company, it was insanely busy, with so many time zones to juggle, and so much litigation and business. Thankfully, we were able to move through that because I didn't want to live my life that way forever. But these habits helped me stay sane, keep my balance, and to engage.

Get Up

The daily habits that I decided to commit to 14 years ago were simple. The first one was to get up early. At the time, I was probably getting up at 8:00 A.M. I didn't go crazy and try to start getting up at 5:00 A.M. I started by getting up at 7:30 A.M. and told myself I was going to do that for 30 days. Then 7:00 A.M. for 30 days. My ultimate goal was to get to 5:00 A.M. and I kept following that pattern until I got there. Today, I set my alarm every day at 5:00 A.M., even if I go to bed late because I still get up to do what I need to do.

Commit to doing something every morning so you get up. For me, I change my voicemail every single morning: "Hey, it's Shawn Meaike, today is Tuesday, September 7th, I'm unable to take your call, leave your name, number, and message." I do that every day so there's no sleeping in, no matter the timezone, no matter what's going on in life. It was my trick to get me up early. I didn't want that feeling in my gut knowing my voicemail said it was Monday, but it was really Tuesday.

My voicemail is never full. Losers have full voicemails. If you interview for your job with me and I call you and it says your voicemail is full, I will never hire you. Same with independent contractors because people that owe money keep their voicemail full.

All my clients had my number and I told them if I don't return their phone call in 24 hours, call and report me dead because only dead people and losers don't return phone calls in 24 hours.

Be Responsive

Which brings me to the next daily habit: I answer and respond to every single call, message, and email. Every single one of them. If you don't want to message someone back, then you should message them and find a way to get them to stop messaging you.

"Hey Tim, who do you work with at the company? Tom? Good. Direct that question to him."

"Hey John, I don't do that anymore. You need to get that information from somebody else. I can't help you."

If they incessantly continue to message you, that's weird. There's a block button—use it.

If you are in business, the phone is your friend. You have to be responsive (except when you need to put it down to be with your family). And by the way, the more responsive you are, the less you have to respond to.

Answer calls by saying, "What's up?" That tends to get people in line because what you're really asking is, "What do you have to tell me? What do you want to share with me? What's the deal?" This will change your life. They'll get to the point and tell you exactly what you need instead of chit-chatting. It doesn't matter who it is, you can change the "what's up" based on who they are and what they say.

Be Healthy

I've never had a six-pack and I'm not trying to get one or tell you that you need one. But I will plead with you to be healthy. Your health is important because you can't do anything else without it, and it doesn't take much to be healthy. You can do something every day to be healthy. Doing something is better than nothing and emotionally and mentally, you'll feel better.

I want to be in good health and live as long as I can. Life is fragile. You never know what's going to happen, but why would I not give it everything I got? We get one shot here as physical human beings.

I like to work out in the morning because another way for me to trick myself into waking up early is to get my workout in before the rest of the lazy human beings roll out of bed. Then I can be done, showered, changed, and ready for the day.

It can be simple decisions too, like being conscious about not overeating. We're unproductive when we overeat anyway. Part of being healthy is staying hydrated. I drink as much water as I can and go to sleep with a bunch of bottles next to me every night.

When you have a job and you have to be there at 8:00 A.M. and you have to leave your house at 7:00 A.M., that means you get up at around 6:00 A.M. to shower. Most people, when they become independent contractors, have no structure and no schedule, and they fail immensely. So, if you're an independent contractor, the good news is you can make your own schedule. The bad news is you make your own schedule. Therefore, you have to find a way to get up early enough, do your workout, get showered, and get changed. Even if you're working out of your house.

The concept that you're going to get rich in your pajamas is false; your pajamas will make you feel like you shouldn't be doing much. You'll be too comfortable. Unless you're somebody who's brilliant, you're a genius and you develop things, you scratch them on a piece of paper and you get rich, cool. But for the rest of us human beings that don't think that way, get up, get showered, and get dressed like you're taking on the day.

Cleanse the Mind

Another habit is that I read the Bible every day. It's the only book I read every day before I go to bed at night. I don't have my phone in my hand. If you call me, then I'm not answering. If you message me, then I'm not answering. For me, it's cleansing and healing. Getting into thought and prayer is something I need to do for myself. You don't need to read the Bible, but it's good for you to get focused and take time out of every day to pause.

Gain Perspective

Every day, I made a decision not to avoid negativity. That was business stuff. I had to deal with it—no complaints. I don't have enough mental capacity to complain. It's a waste of time for me. Life is too precious and I don't want to waste a day complaining.

Instead, what I'm good at is providing myself with perspective. If you need perspective, just look around at what's going on in the world. If you need perspective, just turn on the news and there'll be 6, 8, 10, 25 things immediately that you'll think, damn, things could be so much worse. I'm so much better off than most. I'm so blessed.

Do it Daily

What do you want to accomplish? What are you doing on a daily basis to accomplish it? Right now, write down your daily habits. You might not have any so start with some of mine right now. If you don't want to use mine, that's fine, but then you need some of your own. If you only do it a couple of times, it doesn't make it a daily habit.

Write down what you'd like your daily habits to be and give yourself timeframes—30, 60, 90-day windows— to get there. Outside of that, you're not committed to it. If you say you're going to make a change, start with the next 30 days. I'm not talking about a five-year plan here.

The last thing I want to say to you is to only follow, listen to, and converse with people daily that have actually walked in the shoes you want to walk in—and avoid everybody else like the plague.

6.
REMOVE ALL NEGATIVE INFLUENCES

What is Getting in the Way of Your North Star?

As I've said, my north star is leading, serving, doing things I'm supposed to do, bringing the word of God, living by that, and doing the best I can. Anything that gets in the way of that—that pulls against my mission or journey and/or makes it feel wrong—is a negative influence.

Your negative influences will depend on what your north star is and what's getting in the way of it, so start by asking yourself, what are my goals and objectives? Anything that goes against you getting to your north star is a negative influence.

Once you know what those things are, you have to isolate and remove them as best you can.

Identifying Negative Influences

When I was getting to a point where I wanted to have kids, I realized drinking and using drugs were negative influences on me. Even though I didn't have any kids yet, I didn't want to let them down. That realization put me in a position where I knew that if I didn't remove those things it was going to impede or completely destroy my ability to get to where I wanted to go.

The way in which you speak might be a negative influence in and of itself. Negative influences can also be what you read and listen to.

You're also going to have a lot of people that are negative influences. You may tell them everything, share, and vent, and you may think they're on your side, but they're not. That's because, unfortunately, the majority of people are simply not pulling for you. During your lifetime, you can probably take one hand and count the number of people that are going to pull for you.

Last but not least, you might be your own biggest negative influence. After all, the voice you listen to the most is your own.

Identifying Positive Influences
On the flip side, you need to identify the positive influences. Look for people who are, by nature, positive; those people who tend to be energetic, smile, and are usually in a good mood. You want to replace your negative influences with positive ones.

Life's hard enough; I don't need your help being depressed. Hell, we're all depressed. It depends on the day of the week and what's going on in your life, but we all have crap. That's why I like steady people who tend to stay positive. I don't want to surround myself with people that are always going to say yes, but I want to surround myself with problem solvers, not problem creators.

The Blame Game

When something negative is going on in our lives, we like to tell ourselves it's not our fault. Therefore, we need somebody else to blame, and often find other negative people that love to talk about negativity. Now we have two negative people complaining about how bad everything is and looking for somebody else to blame.

When I got sober, even though I didn't go to AA, I did have a friend tell me that I should make amends to people I'd harmed.

It had been 10 years of this, so I responded with, "That's a long list."

But I did talk to some people and say, "Hey, sorry I did that. I shouldn't have."

While some people said, "Dude, I haven't thought about it," others told me what I had done was one of the meanest things anybody had ever done to them. I just listened and was legitimately crushed.

Those were the things I did from a negative influence standpoint, which is exactly why you have to identify those negative people, songs, books—whatever they are—and get rid of them.

7.
BURY YOUR SH*T IN A BOX

Identify Your Sh*t

Maybe you think the reason you're not doing better, you're sad, or can't get ahead is because of a current or past relationship. Maybe you went through something really traumatic as a kid. Stop letting it stop you.

How do you overcome your sh*t? The first thing you need to do is identify what your sh*t is. Make a list: What are the things that you keep talking about on a daily basis? What do you keep thinking about? What keeps entering your thought process?

Before I got sober, my sh*t was that I wanted to drink and get high. It was my way of life since I was 13 years old. Fast forward 16 years and here I was, making the decision to get sober. I felt I couldn't sleep and was also uncomfortable being around people. Drugs and alcohol meant I could have a lot more fun; they meant not missing out on life. I told myself it was all BS, but that sh*t was in my mind, and it was consuming me.

I had to make the decision that I wasn't going to do that: I wasn't going to drink and get high. That meant if a bunch of my friends were getting together, they were going to drink and get high, and I was going to struggle. Therefore, I found a way to remove myself from those situations. After a year or two, it didn't bother me at all, which meant I could pick and choose where I could go and what I could do.

Put Your Sh*t in a Box

Once you identify what your sh*t is, it's time to ask yourself: What can I do about it today? After all, you don't want your past to dictate the rest of your life.

I've gone through all kinds of sh*t in my life. But when it comes up to the surface, I take it, put it in a box, and bury it. Yes, I'll have to deal with it eventually; I'm not saying that you'll magically be cured.

How do you put it in a box? Remember, all of this sh*t is in your mind, which means if you decide to carve that out and put it in a box, you can. While you can't do it in a day, a week, or even a month, you can make a decision to stop thinking about it.

Decide that your sh*t is no longer going to enter your mental space. Even if you bury 90% of your sh*t in a box and hold onto 10%, you'll be a hell of a lot better off than you were previously.

Redirection & Staying Busy

When you start to think about your sh*t, remind yourself, "Okay, when I start thinking about it, I'm going to think about something else." When I would think about how I wanted a drink, I would instead think about my kids, asking myself, "What can I do better? How can I be a better dad? How can I help them grow?"

You need to train your mind. How do men and women in the military not sleep for three or four days while fighting the enemy? How do doctors open your body up and remove cancerous tissue? How do people perform on a stage in front of 60,000 people while keeping focused? How do 17-year-old kids enter college and play football in front of a hundred thousand people with millions more watching on TV? They have the right mindset, and it's a positive one.

In the beginning, when you're trying to put your sh*t in a box, my advice is to be busier than you've ever been in your life. Find a habit, find a hobby, work out at night, or become a professional archer or an artist. Come up with things to do because idle time is the devil's workshop.

Personally, I never wanted to sleep a third of my life away and then sit the other third of my life away on a couch or chair, thinking about how bad my life was. That's 66% of my life, and it didn't seem like a great existence to me. I didn't want to live that way, so I found other ways to be busy.

When to Deal with Your Sh*t

When should you deal with your sh*t? The short answer is to deal with it later. Whether that's in six months, a year, or even two to five years from now, when you dig up that box, it won't be as bad as you thought it was. Personally, when I decided to unpack some of my own sh*t, I was older and it wasn't nearly as bad as I thought it was when I went through it.

Why is that? Think about it this way: When you think about something on a daily basis—whether that thing is positive or negative—you make it out to be much bigger than it really is. In reality, it's not nearly as good or bad as you thought it was.

Once this stuff's buried, it doesn't mean that everything's going away. You're not going to focus on it and be paralyzed by it, but it doesn't mean your good friend won't ask you about it or you won't discuss it in therapy. Those are things in life that there are options that you have. However, once it's buried, you decide whether you want to still think about it or focus on it.

If moving forward you decide you need to talk about it in another way, do it. But let's say you're in the middle of trying to make a living; you're working three jobs and trying to support your kids and have drama and trauma from the past. Now's not the time to deal with it. But let's say in two years or two months from now, you start to get a little more stabilized and think, I'm not so much in this tragic mode of I can't pay my rent or my mortgage. Maybe I can take a step back now and deal with it.

Think about it like you're at war. Right now your job's just to get everybody out of here alive; there'll be plenty of time to think about things in the future. Trust me. When the bullets aren't flying anymore, you'll get to it, but you've got to bury your sh*t to stay alive right now.

Remember that the greatest healer is time, so sometimes boxing it up, shoving it away, burying it, and putting dirt and stones on top of it is what you need right now. When you decide to dig it up down the road, time will have helped you heal along the way.

What to Do While Your Sh*t is Buried

While your sh*t is buried, your new identity can come into view. What can you do with that productive view? You're not the same person.

You're now the person who can say, "I've gone through stuff, but that's not going to dictate who I am. Those are my trials and tribulations. Those are my scars. It's my journey. I'm supposed to walk in those shoes. I trust the Lord. I got it. I figured out why I'm here."

Once you stop letting circumstances, feelings, family history, etc. dictate who you are, you realize that the past isn't you. You can't do anything about it. There isn't a damn thing you can do about yesterday. Even if you were wrong and you apologize, it still doesn't change anything. It might make you feel better and the other person might appreciate it, but the situation of what you did can't be changed. You have to know, understand, and appreciate that. All you can do is move forward.

After you realize this, the first thing you have to do is forgive yourself, because a lot of us carry the sh*t because we think it's our fault.

Everybody has sh*t. The only people that pretend they don't have any skeletons in the closet are sociopaths. They're dangerous. They're the ones you watch on Dateline. They have nothing wrong with their lives. They're sorry for nothing. They've never made a mistake and they're the perfect person.

When it's buried, leave it buried. Give it time. Don't go try to yank at the thing like a dog digging something up every week. Your sh*t will be there eventually, but the reality is it won't be nearly as bad as you think it is. Time will heal a lot of it. You'll be in a better mental space to deal with it, and your life will be in a better place in general. You'll have some time to say to yourself, "You know what? I'm going to talk to a therapist about this once a week. I'm going to spend some time doing this, and this is going to help me."

But right now, bury that sh*t and go handle your business, because you have no other choice.

8.
SETTING BIG GOALS

Setting IS the Goal

What do you think constitutes a big goal? You probably think you've set a big goal before, and you maybe even reached it. I'm here to tell you—big goals are rarely reached. Only if you did everything perfectly will you reach a big goal. But reaching your big goal isn't what's important. Setting the goal and pursuing it with resilience is.

You're setting goals you think you can accomplish when you really should be setting even bigger goals you probably won't. Why? Because that way you'll get farther than you ever thought possible.

I want you to sit down and think to the end of your life, and ask yourself, what are some of the things I hope that I achieved in my life? I hope that if you stretch yourself and dream big enough, maybe, just maybe, you can achieve them all.

Do you dream big? Do you set big goals? Big goals should be things that you give every mother effing thing to, that you can barely hold on to.

Let's take business goals. For most people, it involves a monetary goal. When I was in my twenties, I wanted to make a hundred thousand dollars a year. When I achieved that, it was then to make a million dollars a year. Seems crazy, right? Well, I did it even though it took me a couple of years to do.

Can I make 10 million a year? And when I made 10…how do I get to be worth a hundred? A billion?

Money doesn't motivate or drive me, but it was a byproduct of doing the right things. My big goals were more about helping hundreds of thousands of people and the monetary goals were a way to put exact numbers to it.

If you're making $150,000 a year right now, a big goal isn't to make $200,000—it's to make a million. You make a million, go make 10. You make 10, go make a hundred. And at some point you'll think, well that's crazy, I can't do that. But the most successful people set goals just like that.

When we launched a life insurance company in 2013, I said we'd be doing a billion dollars in gross revenue annually within our first 10 years. Everybody thought that was crazy. That was a big goal. Now, we're in our ninth year at right around 800 million. As long as we continue to do what we're doing, we'll be a billion-dollar company in our 10th year. But that was a really big goal.

I didn't want to achieve my goals—I wanted to miss them the majority of the time. Because if I did, I knew I was setting them right. I missed my goals six or seven years out of 10 because I set such high goals.

Now, let's say you're making 150 grand a year so you set the big goal to make a million. You miss it and hit $800,000. Hey, $650,000 is still more than you were making, right?

The problem with most of us is we hit our goals because we set the bar so low in everything we do. It could be that your goal is to work 45 hours a week. Well, hell, anyone can work 45. Any self-respecting adult is going to do 40 hours a week, minimally. A big goal means not everyone can do it.

You need to come with a really big mindset and the ability to tune everybody out. I have so many haters on social media who are in their 30s and still live with their moms. Do you think I listen to them? It makes me laugh because it's so stereotypical that it's always the same type of guy trying to come for me. I used to respond to these comments and I'll tell you, everybody's a tough guy from their mama's basement. But then I decided I wasn't going to waste 12 seconds arguing with these people.

Big goals bring out big hate. If you don't have haters, you don't have big goals. If I had launched the company and hoped to do 2 million in sales within 10 years, everyone would've been my biggest fan. The competition would've been my biggest fan.

You need to disrupt things in people. You need to say things that make people around you think you're dumb or crazy or both. You want people to say, "You can't do that."

If you set a goal and people around you say, "Yeah, you can do that," you've set a very, very low bar and a low goal for yourself—and that's sad.

You know people that look at big goals and get scared and think it's too hard? Broke people. They think it's funny that you want to go and do big, outlandish things. Wealthy people don't think it's funny at all. They think it's admirable.

Let broke people hate on you. The more hate, the better. That's the way it's supposed to work. But you have to set such massive goals that everybody around you thinks you've lost your freaking mind. If they agree with you, you're in trouble. If it was that easy, everyone could do it.

Here are the kinds of things you'll hear that shouldn't discourage you. They should let you know you're on the right track:

"That's unrealistic."
"Why do you believe you can do that when you don't know anyone else who has done it?"
"It's not that easy to become a millionaire."
Why don't you understand that you're going to let yourself down?"
"Why don't you set realistic goals and expectations?"
"Who do you think you are? Do you think you're better than us?"
"If it were that easy, everybody would do it."
"I don't want to see you get hurt. I don't want to see you fail."
"Why are you setting yourself up for failure?"

If you're not hearing those things, you better set bigger goals.

A Plan to Achieve

Once you figure out what big looks like to you, you need to figure out how to start achieving them. Extraordinary goals take an extraordinary work ethic, an extraordinary mindset, and the extraordinary ability to keep getting up when knocked down.

For my first real job, they said I needed a master's degree to get promoted. I worked 80 hours a week at my job and went to school at night and finished my master's program in a little over a year. I put in an extraordinary work ethic.

The struggle for most people is believing that those goals are achievable for them. The only difference that separates wealthy people and broke people is that wealthy people believed they can achieve extraordinary goals. The man that says he can and the man that says he can't, they're both right.

To create a plan to achieve your big goals, you have to sit down and write down a detailed plan of how you're going to achieve it; meaning, the steps you have to take action on in order to get there.

But it doesn't stop there. Creating a plan is good and fine, but the actions you need to take to get there are going to affect others and you need their buy-in too. I call them stakeholders. And everybody that has a stake in that decision should be involved.

You need to sit down with all the people in your life that your goals affect. If it's just you, it's just you, but the mistake a lot of people make is they want to, say, leave their job and run their own business and try to make half a million a year, but don't see who else is affected by that and whose help or support you'll need to achieve it.

When I got into the insurance business, I was raising two kids as a single dad. I sat my kids down and said, "Hey guys, here's the deal. You have to understand that I'm going to have to give up time with you to create a business that will be able to give you more in the end."

One note that is just as important: Don't bring in people who aren't involved. You don't need them affecting you.

Really sit down and talk to your family about it. Take a piece of paper and draw a line down the middle of it. On one side, write what you want and need, and on the other, what you're willing to give up to get there. Sit down with the people most important to you and walk through those things.

What I want/need for my family is to be the first guy that made a million dollars a year in my family because I want my family to live without worrying about money. I want my kids to be able to have what they want without worrying about money. You might have to give up some time to get there. Make them understand.

To hear your children say, "Dad, thank you. I know I wouldn't have had this without your hard work," makes it all worth it. Every sleepless night, every seven days a week work week, 16-18 hour days for a year—it makes it all worthwhile just for that.

But you've got to illustrate those things. You have to articulate them and you need to bring the stakeholders in—the people that are involved in your life, your family, your friends, your significant other, anybody out there that has a stake in what you're doing.

You don't need to sell them on it. You just need them to know what you've decided. You're already sold on it so you're doing it. You don't need anyone's permission to have a better life or support your family or whatever it is you're setting out to do.

What you do need to do when you are articulating these things to the stakeholders is you need to share the timeframe in which you're working to achieve these goals.

"I want to make a million dollars a year within 24 months." So I have one year to try and get it right and another to fulfill it. I like giving myself two years for all my big goals, but you can set your own timeframe. I gave myself 10 years to get to a billion because I was starting from zero and I worked out a plan to try and do it.

First, I looked at the industry and I saw that the biggest people in the industry were not even doing a hundred million a year. I didn't think the competition was very good. I knew I could get to a hundred million because nobody had done it yet and it was ripe for the picking. The top people were at 60, 70, 80 million as a company. I knew if I could aim there, I would only go up from there.

The first year we did 12 million, but after that, it skyrocketed. One year we went from 140 million to 400 million. And that's because I saw an opportunity. In life insurance, everyone is a client and we have more leads than we know what to do with. But also, everyone is looking for a second income. I could add more people to my team and bingo, add more volume. And all it would take is whatever I did the first year to do it again, the second year to do it again, and the third year to do it again to double every year.

I knew the first year I'd probably fall short (and I fell way short), but I knew that would keep me grounded. I found the principles that worked each year and just kept working on them. I knew how hard I would work and then I had specific plans regarding regionalization, where in the country we were set up, where we were located, how big to be, how many agents were part-time, full-time, etc. Then I took social media. I knew the only way I could hit the numbers I was looking for was to do it on social media, to get the message out to thousands. At the time, I had like 200 people following me on Instagram. Now, I have 400,000+ following me on Instagram. I knew if I could talk to thousands of people that also had at least a couple thousand followers, I could get my message out to millions of people and then eventually in excess of a hundred million.

It was still a pretty ridiculous goal even giving myself 10 years. But you have to have the confidence that you can do it. Act like you've been there. Stay focused. Don't drink and party it all away.

Make sure your goal is in your face on a regular basis. When I wrote down that I wanted Family First Life to be a billion-dollar company in 10 years, I wrote it everywhere. I put it in my planner every year. Billion-dollar company, billion-dollar company, billion-dollar company. That way, you know what you're trying to achieve and make decisions every day to achieve it.

Also, use public peer pressure. Talk about your big goals.

"Hey, I decided for the next 24 months, I'm going to make a million dollars a year."

"I've decided that I'm going to get wealthy for my family."

"I've decided that I'm going to break that cycle of mediocrity financially for my family."

"I've decided I am that guy/girl that's going to do X."

You have to make these things public. Say it out loud. To your friends, your family, on social media, to the guy that makes your coffee—tell everyone.

And when you do start getting those wins toward achieving your big goals, learn to say, "I'm just getting started."

"Man, I can't believe you did that!"
"I'm just getting started."

Not, "Yeah, I did ok." You have to learn to be able to do that because the minute you start reading your own press clippings, you die figuratively. No matter what you've done, if you can say and have the mindset of 'I'm just getting started,' you will keep achieving.

When you can have that kind of mindset, the people around you will see you and follow you, want to work with you, and emulate you. Because if you go out there and do something nobody in your family's ever done, it'll be a time to celebrate that.

But that time's not now. The majority of the people are going to hope you fail. And honestly, it's because they don't want you to threaten what they're not doing.

There are going to be a few though—not a lot—that are watching and they're going to hope with everything they have in their heart and soul that you succeed. They are going to hope that you're a smashing mother effing success. Because if you are, it gives them hope. They want to believe that somebody they know could do that. They want to believe that somebody they know could change and break some of those generational or cultural cycles.

It's going to feel really good when you start getting where you want to go. Act like you've been there before. Act as if it's just another day. Act as if you belong. I spent a lot of my life acting like I belonged until eventually, I did.

9.
PUNCH IN THE FACE TRAINING

Go Fast, Get Focused

The quicker you get it over with and get punched in the face—literally or figuratively—the better off you'll be.

The first time I got punched in the face by that 8th-grade bully, I knew it was coming. And you know what? I was perfectly fine. I didn't die. The world didn't end. My face didn't fall off. My nose didn't go down my throat.

When I got into sales, what I learned about myself was I wanted to get punched in the face faster than everyone else around me and more than everyone else around me. I was going to develop a thickness of skin that was really going to be hard to compete with.

In real estate, they say you have to come up with your sphere of influence. Your sphere of influence is the people you allegedly know that may or may not buy real estate from you. You're supposed to take all of these people that you know, call them up, and cultivate them as your network.

Now, what most of my friends did was put down maybe five people. They called their mom, aunt, and their two best friends.

That was it. I, on the other hand, made a list of every contact I could find. I called every single person I knew. There was some stupid script, but I didn't use that.

Instead, I would say, "Hey man, did you know I have my real estate license? Listen, I'm a hundred percent sure that I will work my ass off for you. I'll work harder than any real estate agent out there that you could ever find. So if your family or you yourself are buying or selling real estate, you need to utilize me. I'm going to find a way to make sure I not only work the hardest for you, but that I also do the best for you financially."

During this period, I also learned that a typical residential listing paid 6%. If you represented both sides, the buyer and the seller, you kept 6%. If you represented one, the typical split was 50/50, giving you 3%. I was selling houses between $150,000 and $500,000. I realized that money was really tight for those individuals. So I decided I would discount my commission so, if I had both sides, I had 4% instead of 6%. If I had one side, I had 2% instead of 3%. And when I did that, other agents said they wouldn't show my listings because of the smaller cut. I remember saying to my broker, "They will. I know they say they won't now, but they will."

I was right. My volume was so high that there was plenty of money to be made. I did 5 million my first year, part-time. And then it was 15 million the year after that, 20 after that. A little bit of a lot added up. It was a hit at first, but because I took that punch first and fast, it added up and made it worth it.

Within two years, I was the top real estate agent in the office. Then other people started doing the same thing. Meanwhile, I stayed in my lane, learned, and got really good.

What a lot of people do to avoid being punched in the face is they scatter. They try 75 other things, that way they're not really getting punched in the face. They think, I have a residential real estate license, but let's look at commercial and other industries such as rentals, property management and investments, etc. In reality, it's just a way for them to avoid getting punched in the face because they allegedly "have something new" all the time. They just keep running from adversity.

What Happens When You Don't Give a Sh*t
Get punched in the face and fail fast. What happened when I developed this thickness of skin? Over the phone on sales calls, I didn't give a sh*t. I just buzzed through everything and it created this indifference. When people know you don't give a sh*t, they don't want to punch you in the face anymore. When that little bully realizes you're not going to back down, he'll never pick on you again. People around me, no matter the industry I was in, realized they didn't get anything out of punching me in the face anymore because I didn't give a sh*t.

That's a characteristic you can develop and create. You don't have to universally say, "I don't care. It doesn't matter to me. I'm not worried about anything." But once people can feel and know that you don't give a f@#k and they can't do anything to you, you won't get punched in the face anymore.

That doesn't mean people won't still try to emotionally paralyze you. For example, people use litigation as emotional paralysis. They want to shut you down emotionally so you can't do business. When I got sued the first time, that was uncomfortable. But once that happened, I put the paperwork down and eventually found an attorney. I went to sleep and woke up in the morning and realized it wasn't a big deal. Life just keeps moving.

This attitude applies to more than just not getting punched in the face—it applies to getting ahead too. Let's say you've been at your job for four years and you're pretty damn good at it. All these people around you are getting promoted and you're not. Well, ask why:

"Hey, excuse me, Tom, you got a minute. Can we talk in your office? Listen, I'm going to be straight up with you. You know I respect you and have given you four good years of my life, but I have to be honest with you. I should have done this before and that's on me, but here's the thing: I see some people getting promoted and they're not as effective as I am. I'm wondering what has been the basis of the decision to promote them and not me. Do I have the ability to get promoted here? Because the thing I can't live with is having a job where there's no opportunity for growth."

When they start stumbling, don't bail them out—shut your mouth. Remember, you need them to punch you in the face, to explain to you what you're doing wrong. When they ramble for 45 seconds, say nothing. If need be, you can say, "I probably didn't ask the question correctly: Why am I not as good as them? What makes them so much better than me? What would that be? Because I'm just trying to figure this out."

People ask questions in life for two reasons: 1. They're trying to intimidate you, or 2. They're genuinely seeking information. 90% of people don't want to know anything, they just want to bother you verbally.

When someone asks you something, the first thing you have to decide is do they want the information or are they trying to mess with you? And when they're trying to mess with you, which happens to a lot of people, then you have to be willing to get punched in the face.

The other day I was at a meeting with other individuals that run Insurance Marketing Organizations (IMOs) and this guy came up to me and said, "Hey man, nice to meet you. I've heard a lot about you. I've been in the business for 35 years."

I said, "Nice to meet you. Who are you and what organization do you run?"
He said, "I wanted to give you some feedback."

Immediately, I said, "Okay, great. How much volume does your organization do?"

He replied, "What do you mean?"

This is a very weird way to answer a question when you know what the question means—it means you don't want to give the answer.

I just looked at him.

He said, "We do 25 to 30 million a year in paid sales."

I said, "Well, I do 40 million a month. So with all due respect, why would I want your opinion on anything business related? If I wanted to go backward, I would call you. After 35 years, if that's all you've learned how to do, I don't want your advice."

He said, "Well, you don't have to be rude about it."

I said, "I wasn't being rude, I was being honest. I don't need your advice. You can't help me."

The next day, one of the guys that put that meeting together said, "I heard you met this individual and he said he was a little bit taken aback, so I asked what you said to him. When he told me, I told him that you were just shooting him straight and you were right."

A lot of us just don't stop people when they give an unsolicited opinion or they ask us questions. They're looking to bust our behind. Don't give a sh*t about those people.

A part of being willing to be punched in the face is calling people out when they're wasting your time. I drive this H2 Hummer and about once a week when I get gas, someone will always ask me, "How is that on gas?" And I know what they are trying to get at. Either they couldn't afford any kind of car or they're mad I had it. Maybe they thought it was screwing up the world.

I always respond with something like, "Let me ask you something. Why are you asking me that? I'm just wondering, why are you asking me that? Are you busting my ass? Or like, what's up?"

You have to be willing to confront things because a lot of us waste our time answering questions and chasing things into a rabbit hole that doesn't deserve it. Stop giving a sh*t.

Go Fail

When you plow forward and don't have regard for your failing, being embarrassed, getting knocked down, or getting punched in the face, you show your organizational culture that they can follow your fearlessness.

Have crazy goals, be told no over and over and over again, fall on your face, and get back up. Create a culture where everybody around you can embrace the fact that we're not supposed to be perfect. We're supposed to work our asses off. We're supposed to hear the word no a lot. We're supposed to fall down. And most importantly, we're supposed to get the f@#k back up. If you can create that type of culture you can get an army of men and women to work with you and go anywhere with you.

And, as I said earlier, when you start developing that thickness of skin—verbally, emotionally, and physically—the world just seems not to want to mess with you. One thing my mom always told me is you can never get in a fight with somebody smaller, weaker, or younger. But other than that, you gotta do what you gotta do.

How many times can I get punched in the face? How many times can I fall on my face? Most people think failing is falling down. To me, real failing is quitting. I can call a hundred people and if a hundred of them said no to me, I don't think that's failing. I think that's building. If you spend 10 grand to create a marketing campaign and get nothing, you're building your character. You're building your thickness of skin. You're building your business acumen. You're building your intestinal fortitude. So you have to start thinking about where you are today. What am I avoiding?

When you can identify what punches in the face you need to take, you have to identify why you're avoiding those. Why are you avoiding them? Why don't you just go ahead and close your eyes and take it? Why are you not able to take the punch in the face? What are the people watching you going to think?

In the movie Grownups, Adam Sandler's character is bullied as a kid and is perfectly fine with it. Matter of fact, when he ran into Stone Cold Steve Austin's character as an adult, he pushed him around and made fun of him again in front of his wife and his daughter. He dealt with that and he did what most people did: He pretended that it didn't happen. But when he saw his son being bullied, it really hit him that people were watching. So he made a decision to fight him. Stone Cold's character thought everybody expected him to beat Sandler up. But Sandler is now willing to fight. So Stone Cold decides not to.

That clip from the movie is so true. We allow people to treat us a certain way. We have a hard time living with it and we rationalize it. But when you back down, people are watching. When you don't get back up and you cry, people are watching. You have to be careful who's watching, especially if they follow you.

Don't look at falling as failing. Stand up for yourself no matter what because the pain of regret is forever. If you don't, I promise you it will be a thousand times worse than the punch in the face. Because after you take that punch, you'll realize you didn't die and that you're okay. You got it, and that feeling is pretty euphoric. After that, you become pretty powerful and pretty difficult to mess with.

10.
NEVER WORRY ABOUT WHAT OTHER PEOPLE THINK WHY DO YOU CARE?

On a scale of one to 10, how much do you worry about what other people think? The fact that public speaking is the number one fear in the world tells us that a lot of people care about this. It's not jumping out of airplanes, getting eaten by a shark, or getting in a car accident. It's public speaking. Why? Because it's really about getting judged.

Nobody's allowed to judge you and you're not allowed to judge anyone else. If that's the case, then why do you care? What are you worried about? Where does that come from? Why are you worried about what people think?

You think about it whether you're talking to 1 or 10 or a thousand people, or when you put something up on social media. What's funny is people will put things on social media hoping it goes viral, but if I tell them to say it to a group of 50 people, they'd be petrified. You're afraid of the looks on their faces—the judgment.

You have to ask yourself, how uncomfortable are you? If you think you don't care about what people think, think about the last five decisions you made. As you made them, did you think about what other people thought? Be truthful. And did you honestly care? Were you focused on it? Where on that scale of 1 to 10 did you fall?

I think what you'll find is most of the time, we do care what people think in certain circumstances. Your kids, your spouse, your pastor—you want to know what they think.

There's a difference between asking for advice and avoiding judgment. I think you should ask people that have walked before you for advice. They probably know how to do things and they've been through it. And they've probably been punched in the face when they did it. So the reality is, they understand.

But what you have to become laser focused on is not avoiding judgment. Avoiding judgment is avoiding what you think is a punch in the face, but it's actually not.

It's actually very inspiring and empowering for you to say, "You know what? I'm going to do everything I can and do the best I can. I know I'm going to make mistakes. And it's ok."

Most people are afraid of being judged when they make mistakes. If you're really looking to accomplish big goals, you're going to run through life and make mistakes. You're going to move fast and break things. But the reality is most of us are crippled based on the opinions of other people. But are those people qualified? Are they a stakeholder?

If your significant other or your spouse says, "Hey, I have a right to have an opinion about this," they're right. They're not judging you. They have an opinion. They're a stakeholder in your life.

But then you have the ability to say, "Hey, you know what? I appreciate the fact you think I'm working too much, but I have to provide for the kids and help my mom out, and also do this for myself."

You can't make every stakeholder equally happy, so you have to put yourself in a place where you say, "I'm going to make decisions based on the best information I have. I'm not going to make them out of fear. I'm not going to live from a place of fear of failure. And I'm literally not going to give a sh*t."

Why are you so worried about what other people think?

I travel all around the country and share what I do and how I make hundreds of millions a year. At the end, I'll always ask if anyone has questions and 95% of the time, no one will raise their hand for a minute. Then the minute somebody asks a question, I receive 10 more. The first person has to get punched in the face in their world. And guess what? Nobody died. It's asking a question, but being the first person feels like a punch in the face.

I always stop and say, "This is exactly why you are or where you're supposed to be—because you're frozen and you're paralyzed based on caring what other people think.

Can you imagine trying to get ahead while worrying about what other people think? Look at the people that have achieved in their life and look at the things they've done.

I had the pleasure of hearing from one of the founders of Home Depot, Arthur Blank. At the end of the meeting, he asked if we had any questions. So I asked Arthur: What was one of the things that drove him and what advice would he have for me?

He said he pitched this idea to the daughter of the owner of a family hardware store where he had worked for years. He said, "We should buy in bulk, drop prices, and almost have a big box mentality kind of deal."

They actually ended up firing him a while later. Now he didn't have a job so he talked to a bunch of other guys and said, "Why don't we just open up like a big box, warehouse kind of deal? We could go ahead and buy in bulk and sell them at a better price. And eventually, if this thing works we could get really rich. And it would help the consumer because they could buy this stuff for less. We could also teach the consumers some skill sets; bring in qualified people to teach them how to lay carpet and hang sheetrock, things that don't require a permit."

I listened to him share about that and I remember him saying, "A little bit of a lot is a lot. A lot of people in business are very greedy. I wasn't. I knew a little bit of a lot would be more than enough."

He didn't listen to the experts at the hardware store where he worked. Everyone around him was saying he was wrong and shot down his idea, but he wasn't worried about their judgment. He didn't care because he knew he was onto something

He said, "When you're onto something, people tend to push back. So the more resistance I got, the more I thought, I'm onto something. Because if I weren't, no one would care."

Most great ideas in America weren't so unbelievably revolutionary, but they didn't care what other people thought and they didn't stop. A lot of people have the same idea, but what differentiates them from the winners is having the ability or the balls to go ahead and bring it forward. Those people who didn't go for it cared what other people thought.

Think about Uber. It was really revolutionary to disrupt the taxi industry, and yet I've heard so many people say that it was so unbelievably simple.

My response has been, "Dude, it's not usually a great idea. It's a simple idea with a great backbone. Call it what you want, but having the balls to go do it? That's the hard part."

So yeah, you say it's simple and you're right. I agree with you. Launching an Insurance Marketing Organization (IMO) and paying the agents more than anyone has ever paid in the history of insurance, and paying more on bonuses and sharing more of the profits than anyone ever has was not a brilliant idea. But it took a lot of balls to put in place.

Disrupt things. Come up with ideas that people think are crazy and do something about it. Say things that make no sense to other people and don't care about it.

When I listened to Arthur Blank talk about launching Home Depot, he talked about how new of an idea it was. The idea was simple, but the establishment pulled against him. All the hardware stores, the local mom-and-pop shops, were in opposition to big box stores. But what I heard him say was, if it was better for the consumer, both in price and in empowering them to do their own work, then he thought it would be a good business strategy. And it was. But he didn't listen when everybody around him was fighting it.

As matter of fact, if I remember the story correctly, he had two other partners when he started and both of them pretty much said, "Hey man, we're good. We've been doing this now for a while and we're not making the money yet. We think it's not going to work out." And they just got out for what they got into it for. I bet they're kicking themselves.

The Clippers could have drafted Kobe and they didn't. I read it was because of public perception, that he was too young. And they didn't want to be vilified by the press. They gave a sh*t—and that was their issue. The idiot fans and the idiot media have an undeserved opinion. The funny thing about sports is that the media is full of a bunch of guys that didn't play ball and they have an opinion that they don't have the right to have.

The media was saying things like that Kobe was too young, just out of high school, immature, couldn't handle Los Angeles by himself, etc., and that the team needed somebody more seasoned, who was older and went to college.

He had the best pre-draft workout they've ever seen, but they said they were concerned about his ability to handle all this pressure—because that's what the media was saying. They succumbed to public pressure.

"A little bit of a lot will be a lot"
Weaker people ask everyone for their opinions. I'd be rich if I had a nickel for everybody that had a great idea or a great opportunity but passed it up because they were worried about what other people would say about them. I don't want to live my entire life trying to play it safe so as not to piss people off. I'd rather piss people off. That might sound crazy, but if you're not pissing people off, then you're not taking any chances and not disrupting anything.

When I started my Insurance Marketing Organization (IMO), people said I was going to mess things up because of how I structured things. But that was my intent because it's a competitive marketplace. The traditional model is that the IMO keeps a very large percentage of the money. That's not my model.

When I went to the insurance carriers, I said, "Listen, I'm going to pay the agents and the managers considerably more than what everyone else does."

They said, "Are you sure you're going to make enough money?"

I said, "Yes. The traditional IMO is making plenty of money and the agents and managers aren't making enough and can't survive."

My alleged competition said, "Hey Shawn, can't do it that way. We've tried that. We've been doing it for 20, 30, 40, 50 years. Shawn's not keeping enough spread to run a real business. He could have problems. He won't be able to pay for his infrastructure, he won't be able to pay his staffing, he won't pay up his taxes—everything."

I knew they were wrong because they were greedy. They were just scared of my model. But I got that from Arthur Blank's Home Depot model: "A little bit of a lot will be a lot." We're going to make less than everyone else per transaction, but we're going to do so many more transactions than everyone else that we're going to smoke everyone.

A lot of businesses think they will win just because they've been around longer. But me? I'm going to come in, knock you in the mouth, knock you out of the way, step out and step on you and compete to make sure the consumer does better and the employee or independent contractor does better. What I mean by that is when you launch a company and you decide to give back more to those stakeholders—your employees, your independent contractors, your clients—and keep less for yourself, you will beat those guys.

I did that in real estate. Prior to when I started, this whole "For Sale By Owner" (FSBO) started. Men and women all over the country utilized the internet and started marketing like crazy and basically said to homeowners, if you go through us, we'll market your property. They are doing it for flat fees saying, instead of you paying 6% to real estate agents, you can pay us 500 bucks. So if the house is a hundred grand, instead of paying $6,000, you can pay $500.

My peers said, "That's the dumbest idea ever. It'll never work."

But I wasn't so sure.

The agents and brokers I knew said, "Shawn, it will never last because they don't have access to the MLS," which is where all agents list a house.

But I thought eventually, that wasn't going to be enough. That's why places like Realtor.com just weren't on top of it. So many people got into their business that wouldn't have gotten in had they been out in front of it. If these national realtors had utilized the internet better, there wouldn't even have even been a competition.

I always look at the competition and what people are doing. I never immediately think, That's so stupid. It'll never work. Now it might be dumb and if it's dumb, I'll tell you and I'll tell you why. But these guys automatically just thought that what they did was perfect.

Nobody has the perfect business. Nobody. And you can see businesses every single day that somebody else replicates, tweaks, and then does better than the person that originally did it. You gotta be really far out in front to not worry.

Me? I pay attention. I bet Amazon every day, as big as they are, is thinking somebody else could do this. I bet they always think, We need to keep getting more warehouses and trucks and a bigger presence on the internet and more stock and better contracts. That's business.

Find a need and fill it and fill it with better quality and a better financial opportunity for others, whether they're working for you or they're a client. If you believe in what you're doing, believe it. You have the right to change your mind, but don't let it be because you care what other people think.

What Happens When You Don't Care

Even if you know you need to stop caring what other people think, it's easier said than done.

A big thing you can do is to get ahead of it and stop it before it starts. What I started doing in meetings was as soon as I walked in, I set the stage for what we're going to talk about, the structure. I go over that first, and then I let whether it's the 10 or 10,000 people I'm talking to know that I can see them.

I literally say, "I can see you all like you can see me. So if you don't want to be here, you don't need to be."

Then I say, "Don't be upset about this, but I don't give a sh*t what any of you think."

My goal is to help, serve, and educate. I am very focused on helping people get to a better place. And I never talk about what I don't know. But I can only do that if I don't care what other people think and I let them know that to clear the air and stop it before it starts. Then we're all on the same page and we can actually have an honest conversation. Because I won't be worried about what the dude in the fourth row thinks. I don't focus on that so I can instead be focused on what matters.

When you start saying that enough, out loud, and you start explaining it to people, whether you're on a Zoom, in a meeting, or you're speaking in front of a small or big group, you empower people to do the same. You actually talk yourself into not caring. It's a self-fulfilling prophecy.

When people come to talk to me and I can tell they're nervous, I ask them why. They might try to say they aren't, but I always press them and it's always about not wanting to screw up.

I ask, "Are you going to give it everything you got?" Yes. "Are you qualified?" Yes. "Then how can you screw it up? It will either resonate with people or it won't, but you shouldn't care about that."

When I started speaking, my north star was making a difference in people's lives. I've been through a lot of sh*t, failed a lot, been punched in the face a lot, punched back, and kept getting up and I can share those experiences to help people. I can get people to understand that it isn't complicated. That comes from a lack of fear of being judged. People say all kinds of things about me and I don't care.

I got into a few different businesses where people would say things like, "the client's going to buy or die." That made no sense to me and I wasn't going to do that.

For example, in life insurance, I was all about pushing as hard as I could because everybody has to have it and they get harmed by not having it. But some of these other things that I would sell back in the day, it wasn't buy or die, it wasn't life or death. I did work hard. I did want to make money. I did want to make my commissions. But I wasn't going to sell somebody a $400,000 house when I was a hundred percent sure they shouldn't buy one over 200 grand.

I was in a closing one time for a condo I sold a guy and his pregnant wife. It was about $194,000, give or take. As he was signing the mortgage documents, I looked at the closing documents and saw what was going to happen with the interest rate. And I saw that the loan was going to implode. He could never maintain the payment after the first year.

I said, "Don't sign that."

And I was the seller's agent! I wouldn't have cared if the sale was worth 200 grand or 200 million. I wasn't going to harm them. I knew they wouldn't be able to pay the mortgage. I had to speak my mind. I will be judged for that by some people and I still don't care.

If I decide to go do something, I'm going to do it. If you think it's weird, I don't care. I'm going to live my life to the best I can by God and make the best decisions I can. That's it. My north star is to do right by God, my family, and all of the people I work for and serve; otherwise, I don't care. I'm not messing with it.

But you have to make that decision for yourself. Care about what matters and don't care about the rest. Everybody wants to do the right thing when it's easy, but doing the right thing when all the odds are against you is what counts.

Make that decision today to stop caring. If it makes you feel better, it's in the Bible that no one has the right to judge you and you don't have the right to judge anyone. So stop caring and stop judging. But when you start to notice how much you judge, it's hard to stop. But you can't judge and ask not to be judged. You have to take that inventory every day of how much you're judging and how much you're caring. Take inventory over the next 24 hours of those two things and you'll see. But keep trying and keep taking inventory and you'll find you care less and less and judge less and less because you don't care.

Stop judging people yourself, and then you can ask not to be judged and be public about it and talk about it. It's a self-fulfilling prophecy. The more you tell people you don't care, the less you will. Tell yourself daily: "I'm going to make the decisions I'm going to make. I'm going to do the best I can on a daily basis. I'm not going to live in fear and be paralyzed by others' opinions of me. People are always going to have an opinion. Who cares?"

In other words, you can't ask people not to judge you when you judge everybody else, so you have to make a decision. You can't have it both ways. I'm not judging you for what you believe in. As long as what you're doing is legal and ethical and you're not bothering anyone, that's fine.

Start saying to your colleagues, "Hey, let's be clear about something: We're going to coexist. We're going to work together. We're not going to be judgemental; in fact, I'm not going to judge any of you."

If you make that a public statement, then you can set clear expectations and focus on what really matters instead of worrying about nonsense all the time.

11.
NEVER TAKE A STEP BACKWARDS—NO RETREAT

Always Move Forward

At the end of the day, life is hard. At the end of the day, business can be hard. At the end of the day, everything can be hard. But what I think makes it nearly impossible to live is taking a step backward every time it gets hard. There's a lot of glory and respect to getting knocked around all day long, but there's never any to going backward. You may not have gone forwards—hell, maybe a recession hits—but you held the line. You barely grew, maybe less than half a percent; but, you didn't go backward.

Life, success, business, parenting—all of it is a marathon and not a sprint. At the end of each day, as long as I never went backward and always moved forward, I knew I was going to be fine. You're only faced with a decision to go forwards or backward when it gets hard. When it's easy, you're just walking. There are no crossroads, there's no forwards. You're just walking through your life. But when the sh*t hits the fan or when it gets even a little hard, you start to question yourself, feeling like you don't know what you're doing, you have two choices: move forward or go backward. I'm telling you, you can't go backward. Taking a step backward at any level is just quitting. If you believe in what you're doing, you can't retreat and run backward. This is why I keep the mindset to always move forward.

When you start calling it retreating, it never sounds good. Even if I walked out of my house and there were 12 dudes with ARs and I didn't have a bulletproof vest or a gun, and there was something to stand up for—like kids out there, women that were being hurt, people being taken advantage of—I'm going to fight. Moving forward doesn't mean living recklessly or doing stupid stuff in life, but when you make a decision and life is hard and you're going forward, it is a fight.

I was on a podcast one day, and the guy asked what I would do if I was walking through a bar and a guy slapped my girl on the behind. I said I would beat the crap out of that guy.

He responded, "Well, there are ramifications for that. Then you can get in trouble and get arrested."

But I said, "He assaulted her first, so I'm pretty sure I wouldn't go to jail for defending her. And on top of it, I have to sleep at night and wake up the next morning knowing I did the right thing."

When you're moving forward, it's not necessarily reckless, but it can be somewhat uncomfortable. A lot of people choose to retreat though. That's why I knew that if I never took a step backward, I'd eventually end up further along than other people. Even if they have a better day, better week, better month, better quarter, or better year, I'd always move forward and eventually outpace them all.

I've kept that mentality and movement with everything I've done. You've gathered by now that I am a big fan of goals. When everything goes perfectly and I work my ass off and I'm so tired at the end of every day, I'll eventually reach my goals. But goals allow people to be very unproductive. What I mean by that is it's like a salary or a bonus or an earn-out—people get parameters for their goals. Then all of a sudden they're two months in and realize they can't hit their goal, so they stop caring and say, "I can't hit it anyway." I don't care if I'm nine months in or even 11 months in. I'm always trying, at least hitting my drop-dead goals.

When I decided to get in better shape, I said I wanted to work out seven days a week. The problem with hard goals is something always comes up. There could be a day I was traveling or didn't get sleep the night before. In these situations, I create a drop-dead goal: I'm going to work out four days a week no matter what happens in the world. I am still going to go for seven, but I'm definitely not doing anything less than four. A lot of us set goals and they're aggressive, but then two months in we're still not hitting them. So what do we do? We give up because we were only doing it based on that goal in the first place.

In my first year running a life insurance business, my goal was for the company to issue a $15 million minimum. But then I said, you know what? We might not do it. So I'm going to work my ass off, but the drop-dead goal is $10 million. I still focused on $15 million, but I didn't want to be discouraged if we didn't quite get there because $10 million was pretty solid too. Because there are going to be some bumps in the road, but you're still not going to let yourself get below a certain threshold.

My drop-dead goal has always been tied to not going backward financially. I might have really aggressive, crazy, over-the-top goals, but my drop-dead goals are just as important. I'll never go backward on them. Everybody laughs about New Year's resolutions because most people set stuff up they really probably can't hit and they don't get wins. Wins are important. Wins add up. If you want to give yourself small wins, add some drop-dead goals. They're the better measuring stick.

When I was playing football at eight or nine years old, I remember being on defense. It was one of the first practices that we had full gear on. I was playing inside linebacker and the ball was snapped. I was sliding backward a little bit when someone pushed me in the back. I thought it was one of my teammates, but it was my coach.

When I spun around, he said, "Don't ever go backward, always lateral or forwards."

He spent the first few weeks standing behind the four of us linebackers. He said, "You can't play this position backpedaling. You're going to be relied on."

If you look at that defensive scheme, the linemen do a lot of the work: They hit people, keep them off of you, and make a lot of tackles. But they make those tackles moving forward, not six, seven yards deep; that'd be a first down every two plays.

My coach said to me, "Playing linebacker is like being successful in life. The reason some of these guys aren't going to be successful and I think you will is that you don't give an inch. You don't take a step backward. You're not afraid. It doesn't mean you're the most talented person I've ever coached in my entire life, but you're always moving forward."

It turned out he didn't need to put his hand on my back much. But some of these other guys, he would do it for a day or a week and then he would just get somebody else in there. It was a good lesson in life. I wasn't afraid of getting hit by the ball or by people. I realized at this young age that I was willing to do things that most people around me weren't willing to do. It wasn't because I was superior in any way. I just wasn't scared, and it let me play better.

When you live always going forward, people want to follow you. Everyone wants to be an unbelievable leader, but leadership happens naturally. If your goal in life is to be a great leader, you don't understand leadership. Your goal in life should be to be a great servant of people, to live with a servant's heart, to do right by people, work your ass off for them, and empower them.

Most people inherently have fears; when you can show them that you're fearless, they may not change everything about themselves, but they're watching you and watching you get knocked around.

Once I was asked, "What's the greatest gift that you gave your agents when you were training them?"

I tell them that once I went on the phone in front of them and made dials. Some people on these calls cussed me out. It got to the point where some of my agents were telling me, "You'll get the next one."

Even though I was already making half a million dollars a year, they were still pulling for me. They saw me fail but my fearlessness showed them that it was okay.

I want to live the way the Bible says, to live forward, facing and falling forward, and getting back up. I don't take a step backward because I don't want God, my kids, or my coworkers to see me retreat. I didn't want anybody to see me retreat. And I also knew that a lot of people were inclined to retreat. If you move forward, get punched in the face, get back up, move forward, get punched in the face, and get back up again, you're going to be much further ahead in life.

How To Not Go Backward

Understand the bigger purpose again: What is your north star? Keeping that in mind will help ensure you never retreat. If you're following your north star, retreating isn't even a possibility. You would never give up, show cowardice, or back down when you're living from your north star. It's not possible.

And in life, business or personal, whatever you're doing, once people around you know you don't retreat or give in, that you'll stand up for yourself, they'll leave you alone. People do terrible things to people and they victimize and you can't prevent everything, but you need to live for yourself anyway. It's not about being the biggest, baddest person but about not having fear because you always know you're going to be moving forward, always toward your goals. That mentality helps dissipate fear. You're just not afraid of getting punched in the face.

The greatest gift you can give me as a salesperson is a lack of fear. When people look you in the eyes and see how serious you are, they'll see you don't have any fear and it's not about you making the sale—it's about them. When you do that, I don't give a damn what you're selling, they're going to buy it.

I'm a big fan of selling things people need, not things they want. But give me any product and tell me what you're pitching and I will sell the crap out of it because I don't care about being punched in the face. People can see that and it disseminates the tension of making the sale and now the magic is there instead. Because my north star is providing for my family and serving other people and I never forget that when I'm selling.

There's something magical that happens with companies and movements when it's always about that north star and moving forward, not about the sale. It's what moves things forward, not backward, and there's massive power behind that.

When you're making a decision about retreating or moving forward, ask yourself: How passionate am I about what I'm talking about? Because if it's something you don't care about—like two guys of similar size in the parking lot that want to fight—there's no need to become involved. I'm not retreating. It just has nothing to do with my north star and what I'm about. But a grown man and a kid? You better believe I'm not retreating and will be stepping in.

When you get into a fight—literally and figuratively—you learn.

"I should put my hands up there. I should hit him here. Sh*t, that didn't work."

Regret doesn't happen when you fight for what you know is right, even if you get punched in the face. It happens when you back down, and that regret will last a lifetime. And the elation of moving forward and refusing to back down will give you a success that you probably never thought was possible. If you can live in that, regardless of what you're doing in life, if you fight when you need to because it means you're moving forward, you're going to have a very successful life. You'll be shocked at how fast and how far you can move ahead when you have a complete, unadulterated refusal to take a step backward.

Think about the person behind you like my coach was; your spouse, your kids, your best friend, your pastor, your mom. Imagine those people standing behind you, making sure you never go backward, telling you that you can do it. It's that strength you can call upon when you get punched in the face, because you will get punched in the face, and for the most part, you're going to be okay.

When I started my life insurance career, they gave me leads and I went into the field. My kids were seven and five at the time and I was on like my third or fourth appointment. I hadn't closed at all that day, and I remember thinking to myself, If I leave here, I wasted an hour driving out. I can't support my kids doing that. And I felt like my kids had their little hands on my back and if I went backward, I would knock them over. I never forgot that.

I went to that sales call and said I wanted to know more about their current policy because I didn't want to let them down. I ended up finding out that their terms both ended in a couple of months, wrote them some policies, and made myself around $4,000 for an hour's worth of work.

Sometimes you need people around you to physically help you. Find other people that have been where you want to go. All I do is find people that have done things that I want to do and I pick their brains. Part of what I ask them is to tell me two or three times when they thought about quitting, retreating, or going backward and how they responded. It's incredibly helpful when you're faced with similar obstacles.

Especially if you're in sales, be an information gatherer. Every time you meet people, watch what they say and do and how they say it and how they do it. When you're at a business meeting or a dinner, watch how people interact with your children. Look at their nonverbal listening skills, interactions, what they say when they greet people, and what all that looks like. If you're not paying attention to that, that's a special kind of stupid. That's how you get beat. But when you really watch people and see what they need and who they really are, you'll have everything you need. The rest of it is like a hot knife on butter.

If you find that you did retreat, and it gave you a pit in your stomach and a sickness, here's the good news: Go make a decision not to retreat anymore and live in that. That sickness will go away and you'll start to feel elation. You'll start to chase it like a healthy drug and avoid the sickness. You'll never go backward anymore, not care what other people think, not care about getting punched in the face, because you'll choose elation over the sickness any day.

People are always watching. When I talk to somebody in sales that isn't willing to get uncomfortable, I say, "You know, your kids are watching, right? Is this what you really want to model for them?"

Know you're going to be okay and know that other people are watching and they're hoping they could be as fearless as you.

12.

LIVE BY THE STANDARDS: "I AM HUMBLE, I HAVE NO FEAR AND EVERY DAY IS GREAT"

Be Humble

Be humble, have no fear, and every day's a great day. Those are three things I've always tried to live by on a daily basis. What are three things that you live by on a daily basis? They can be good or bad, positive or negative. Have they helped you? Have they been detrimental?

Let's start with the first of my three things: Be humble. I've always been a fan of humility because if you're not humble, you're going to be humbled. The minute you start thinking you're extra special, you'll be taught very quickly that you're a human being like the rest of us. The minute you have success and start bragging about how great you are is the minute you'll be brought back down to earth. Personally, I'd rather stay humble than be humbled. If Jesus can wash feet, you can be humble in your success.

Think of it this way: Do you enjoy people telling you how great they are? When it comes to all the people you've worked for, that have coached you and led you, if they lacked humility, you probably didn't enjoy playing or working for them. I think the only leaders that people follow are those with humility.

Have No Fear

How do you become fearless? You face situations that are fearful. Then, after a while, you realize none of it is really a big deal.

When you say you're afraid, what does that really mean?

For example, if someone tells me they're afraid of heights, I dig deeper:

"When I'm up there, I'm scared of falling and getting hurt."

"Okay. Got it. Now let's talk about when you're up there, the odds or the probability you would fall. It's pretty slim, right?"

At the end of the day, you have to rationalize what the fear is because then it's gone. Let's use another common example: The fear of public speaking:

"I'm scared that I won't do a good job, that people will laugh."

"Why would that happen?"
"I could say the wrong thing."

"Okay, well, first of all, start thinking about what you want to say, and also remember you can't make everybody feel the way you want them to feel. You're not going to get everybody to appreciate what you're saying."

You have to be willing to not care. Stop being guided by what you think everybody else thinks. Once you're there, then every day's a great day right now.

Every Day is a Great Day

When you wake up in the morning, earlier than most people, you already feel better about yourself because you're up and getting sh*t done. You don't have to get up at three o'clock in the morning to do that; hell, you get up at six and beat most people.

But what if you also start saying, "Today's going to be a great day"?

The mind is a powerful thing and it eats what we feed it. For me, I was more worried about feeding my mind more appropriately than my body; it took me a long time to realize I needed to start eating better and watch what I put in my body because I want to live longer and I don't want to look terrible. But from a young age, I knew I couldn't let my mind be fed the wrong nutrients, and a big part of that is perspective. So why not have the perspective that today is going to be great?

You woke up, you're alive. God allowed you to wake up another day, which means it would be disrespectful not to do everything you could to make it the best day ever, right? To take advantage of that situation, to be in a place where you can win, where you're going to achieve, and be around successful people. It's not about money, it's about decisions.

It's crazy when you know the greatest things in life aren't material things: cars, houses, planes, and boats. Those are cool—don't get me wrong—but it's knowing that if your kids need something medically, you don't have to ask, that's real achievement. If insurance doesn't cover it, you can pay for it. If your kid's qualified to attend a prestigious school, you're good, you can pay for it. You have more than enough money coming in. When you can get there, everything changes—and I mean everything.

Yes, money's important to the quality of your life, and you experience this when your kids can go to pick something up at the pharmacist that's not covered by insurance. Those are the wins during the day that you have to hold onto. Those are the wins during the day where you have to say, "You know what? That was a big deal. That felt good. I'm glad I did it. I appreciate that. I'm going to be better off in the future."

Another reason I wanted to make money and be financially successful was I wanted to give money back. In fact, one of the things I take the most pride in outside of being able to provide for my family is the fact that when other people are in need and looking for somebody that can help, they know they can call me.

But don't forget, you have to have a perspective of humility in order to be fearless and have a great day. When somebody asks you how your day is, instead of saying, "Ah, it's okay," or, "It's been better," you should be saying, "It's freaking great," or "It couldn't be any better."

If by nature you're whiny, wherever you're working isn't going to be a good place for you to work. And by the way, that's okay, you don't have to be a good fit for every employer or every job. But you do choose to have a great day and you choose to have a bad day, and that's where people get stuck. It's not by accident if the day is good or bad—it's your reaction to the stuff that makes it so.

Now, there are things that people go through that are unimaginable. But when we start to have enough perspective and people say they had a terrible week of sales, you can respond with, "But are you dying of cancer? No? Then come on, dude."

That same bad perspective comes into play when people say they're in a slump. There's no such thing as a slump. A slump is you scapegoating your lack of results as if it's literally outside of your control. Are you working as hard as you did last week? Are you working more hours? Are you playing the numbers game? Did you double the number of appointments you made? Did you double the activity you had? Did you double the calls? Did you double your door knocks? At the end of the day, the whole thing is a numbers game, and if you want to set yourself up to win, all you have to do is stack the deck with activity.

If you're in a "slump," you need to figure sh*t out now personally, emotionally, and physically or go look for a new team because you're going to be out.

However, when you choose to live with these three core principles, then you'll become very successful whenever you choose to be successful.

13.

STAND UP FOR OTHERS WHO CAN'T STAND UP FOR THEMSELVES

You're Either a Wolf, A Sheep, or a Sheepdog

I read that there are three things you can be in life: a wolf, a sheep, or a sheepdog. There are wolves everywhere, so you need to learn to identify them. Wolves could be your best friend, your employer, anybody. Sheep need sheepdogs to stand up to the wolves.

In elementary school, there was a kid in my class with cerebral palsy. It wasn't his fault, but physically he would've fallen into the category of sheep simply because he couldn't run or communicate like the rest of the kids. He was severely disabled. The wolves in our school would pick on him, make fun of him, say stupid stuff, and mimic him when he walked. And then there were sheepdogs like me who would stand up for him. Sheepdogs are not people that go looking for trouble. They just stand up when they see people that can't stand up for themselves.

It doesn't matter how big the wolves are. Sheepdogs stand up for the sheep simply because it's the right thing to do. And if you're willing to be a sheepdog in life, you're willing to take a punch.

I've needed people to stand up for me in my life. We all do. Not only does everybody need somebody to stand up for them at some point in time, everybody should have stood up for somebody at some point in time. The problem is a lot of people make the decision not to because people are weak and standing up is hard.

The majority of people out there are sheep or wolves and a lot of them are sheep trying to be wolves. Standing up for people is hard because wolves do best in a pack, so being a sheepdog often means standing up to them all. You're outnumbered. How many hidden camera shows have you seen where somebody's being harassed in the street and they watch 27 people walk by the girl and nobody does anything?

It's human nature nowadays; people don't want to get involved. When my daughter was three weeks old, we didn't live in a great area. I was sitting outside with her and her mother and there was a couple outside next door arguing and he punched her in the face. I jumped right up and started wailing on him. Either the cops were called or they were driving by, but they came and sorted it out. They arrested the guy, but they warned me about getting involved in certain situations because they could have seen me punching a guy and accidentally arrested me. I wasn't trying to be a hero. I just saw a lady getting punched by a man and I'm a sheepdog. That was it. I don't just stand up for people if all the circumstances are perfect or I will only run out and help you as long as it's not cold, wet, and dangerous. You're either a sheep, a wolf, or a sheepdog—and nothing in between.

Being Fearless Means Getting Punched in the Face for Others

Don't make decisions based on whether or not other people will get mad. You make decisions in life from conversations around you. Maybe at work, you hear people talking about a guy who isn't great at math, and people start saying he's not smart, but you know he's great at organization. What does it cost you to speak up?

Everyone is talking sh*t about everyone else. Yes, people are talking sh*t about you. So why not knock it off? When you speak up for others, that's standing up for the culture of your company too.

The people on my team are on my team. It doesn't matter who they are; they're on my team. I will stand up for anyone on my team and it doesn't matter why. Because the whole point of a team is if there's an incident or a problem and somebody does something to harm somebody on your team, you stand up for them. You're stronger together.

If my brother calls me up and says, "Hey man, I have a problem," I drive down to where he is.

If he's in the parking lot with three guys and he's fighting, I don't stop and go, "Hey wait a minute, what are y'all fighting about?"

I don't give a sh*t what they're fighting about. I jump in and defend my brother.

If my buddy's wife is in the grocery store and something happens, I don't go, "Well what happened?" I intervene and I protect her.

That's what a team does. It matters because without that there is no team, family, business partners, or any real relationships. If you're my business partner and somebody attacks you, I defend you. I don't ask you what happened. I might afterward, but not at that moment.

You need to have the back of anyone on your team. And if your friends or your family or anyone on your team is doing stupid stuff, then you shouldn't be hanging out with them.

In my last year in high school, we did our first day of hitting drills and this guy on my football team got absolutely annihilated. He was a nice guy and I got no joy out of hitting him, but he was always down.

In the locker room, I said, "Hey dude, I'm not trying to be difficult, but why are you here? I have no problem doing this, but the coaches are going to keep doing this to you. I know you're not trying to slow everybody down and I'm not mad at you, but why are you here? Are you enjoying this?"

If he told me he was enjoying this, that would have been the end of it. But he didn't say that.

"I don't enjoy it all Shawn," he said. "Like at all."

"Then why are you doing it?" I asked.

"Well, my dad wants me to."

"Why do you care about what your dad wants?"

"I don't want to let him down."

"Does he know you don't like it?"

"Yes."

"If I were you, I'd tell my dad to f@#k off. But you gotta do what you gotta do."

    I couldn't tell his Dad to f@#k off, but I could stand up for him by encouraging him to take a stand. And eventually, he did. He quit football. Still, I wish I had said something to my coaches. Was I afraid of my coaches? Yes. Would they punch me in the face? Yes (with a helmet on). I wasn't afraid to be punched in the face on the field, but I was cowardly at that moment.
    What I should have said to my coaches when they were having him get hit over and over was, "Y'all made your point coach. He's not sucking on purpose. He's just not any good."

    The regret comes from not standing up for other people, not saying, "Man, I wish I would have made fun of that person."

    The people talking sh*t—the wolves—we should line people like that up and have a conversation with them. I remember thinking my family would whoop my ass if I were a wolf. Wolves just take advantage of the sheep, pick on them, torment them, and attack them. And the sheep allow themselves to be attacked. There are certain things you can't control, like someone bigger attacking you. You didn't allow it to happen, but now what? What did you do that allowed the attack? It doesn't necessarily mean that wolves are physically intimidating, but when you're in a room full of people and one or two people who aren't in that room are being spoken about because they're perceived to be weaker, everybody laughing and participating in that room is a wolf.

Be a sheepdog; stand up for what's right, even if you're the only one in the room doing it.

You don't want to be a sheep. You're going to stand up for yourself. Because regardless of the outcome, what I will tell you is the more you stand up for yourself in any situation, the less people bother you.

When I got into real estate, there were a lot of wolves that wanted to steal money by not paying rent. I let everyone know I was a sheepdog, not a sheep. You don't pay the rent, I'll be here. I'm going to be knocking on that door at 4:00 A.M., calling you at 5:00 A.M., doing an inspection at 6:00 A.M., and doing a welfare check on your child at 7:00 A.M. I'm going to be your worst enemy.

It's not about violence and fighting. It's about standing up for what matters. That's what sheepdogs do, even if it means getting punched in the face while doing it.

If you're launching a business, how good is it going to be for the people you employ? How good is it going to be for the people you serve? Your clients? The people you sell to? The local economy? Society?

When I started my life insurance business, we decided to treat people better than they had been treated, historically. We paid them better, gave them better opportunities to grow, better benefits, and a better ability to win long term. I always wanted my employees to be so well paid that if they even thought about trying to get another job or they got mad one day, I wanted them to say, "Damn I'm pissed today, but I'll be giving up 50% of my salary if I go somewhere else."

I believe in paying people well and sharing the profits. That's standing up for other people. There are companies that make hundreds of thousands of dollars a damn minute who don't have as many six-to-seven-figure income employees as we've created at my companies. And we didn't make anywhere near the money those companies made, but we stood for people, and that allowed them to stand up for themselves.

14.
TIME TO MOVE FAST

You Must Move Fast to Win

Ask yourself: Are you moving fast in the game of life?

Professionally, I think probably 60% of people move slowly, 30% move at average speed, and 10% move fast.

The speed at which you move will be a motivator for the people around you and it will also separate you. The saying "move fast and break things" is a good slogan for startup companies. I still live by it today and we're in our insurance company's 10th year.

If you don't move fast and I do, I'm also going to beat you. If you're an entrepreneur, you will get left behind. If you work in sales, you won't get it.

There's an old saying in sales that the minute you hire a salesperson that you're supposed to train, you make money. The minute you hire anyone, whether that be an employee or independent contractor, you give up your right to be average and ordinary.

I was talking to a guy who was in the NFL for a bit (we went to the police academy together) and asked him, "What was the most eye-opening moment?"

He said it was when he got into his first preseason game in the huddle. The guys told him, "Listen, this is how we make a living."

Basically, they told him not to f*ck it up. You might be a rookie, but this isn't college anymore. They all feed their families based on how they perform on the field, and your performance will affect theirs. He said it was very sobering because he realized how serious this was. When you're playing ball in college and high school you're not getting paid, but now all of a sudden you're a professional and your performance affects other people. And those people are going to stand up for their income, their families, the whole deal. They're trying to make the team and get paid.

The same goes for when you're an employee or an independent contractor: the minute someone is relying on you and you hire some people or you get promoted, now people are relying on you to make an income. When other people are relying on you for their income, you give up your right to be average and ordinary. That means you're going to have tough days. Sure, you're making more money, but with that reward comes a burden. Good leaders are not average and ordinary people because they get that burden. Nobody trying to feed their family is inspired by the average and ordinary.

If you become part of the fast 10%, there's so much out there for you. Why? Because a hundred percent of it's available, and only 10% of the population's chasing it. The world really is your oyster. You can achieve whatever the hell you want to achieve because you're really not competing with anyone else.

When I get up in the morning at 4:30 or 5:00 A.M. and you get up at 7:00 A.M., I'm already that far in front of you; too far ahead. Why am I good at sales? I get up at 5:00 A..M., work out, get my stuff ready for the day, deal with the people I sold to the day before, deal with the administrative sh*t, and by 8:00 A.M., I'm on the road. I've accomplished stuff in three hours that you're trying to get done during the day.

If it's 1:00 P.M. and you're at the gym, what are you doing? Those are prime earning hours, prime productivity hours. You know, what's great about being in the gym at five o'clock in the morning? You're not making sales calls at 5:00 AM. So from 5:00 to 6:00 A.M., you didn't miss anything. Nobody's trying to buy a car, a policy, or a house at 6:00 A.M., so get all your crap done before the day starts. That's how you move fast.

What's Slowing You Down?

What are those things that are inhibiting your ability to move fast? In the game of business, we all have the same ability to run fast…so what is holding you back from running fast? Is it personal relationships? Is it professional? Is it your mom? Your dad? Your significant other? The business you're in? Are you getting up late? Is it alcohol? Are you eating like crap? Are you ignoring your health? What are the things that are slowing you down or not allowing you to move fast? Because sometimes you're just breaking things and you're moving slowly. You're kind of just spinning, which is the worst. When you're not moving fast, you're breaking a bunch of sh*t, but you're not breaking the good stuff.

When you're moving fast, you're going to get punched in the face. You're going to say, "Man, I didn't see that coming." Maybe you missed a client or a sale, but you're moving fast so you have 12 more appointments today.

Personally, I never want to be involved in paralysis by analysis. What happens is a lot of people avoid being punched in the face, thinking "Let me overanalyze this thing so I can be a hundred percent sure I won't get punched in the face." Well, if you're a hundred percent sure you're not going to be punched in the face, I'm a hundred percent sure you're not going to be successful.

Default to Aggressive

You always have to default to aggressive. Why? Because being aggressive gets you moving faster. Be aggressive asking for the sale, telling a client what they need to do, and helping an agent.

When I was driving to the office at 5:00 A.M. and everyone's house was dark, all I ever thought as I drove by each one was, "You can't beat me. You can't beat me. You can't beat me either."

I don't care who I'm competing with—they can't beat me. Give me two hours a day, 14 hours a week. It doesn't require talent—you still can't keep up. That's why I always wanted to move fast: I knew that if I had a good work ethic and worked my ass off, the people around me would respect me.

Lead from the Front

Are you leading from the front? Leading from the front isn't about being perfect, but about running faster than the people you're working with. It's about leading, working harder, and being the hardest worker in the room. The one thing I can promise you is nobody will outwork me, no matter who they are or what company they run. They'll never, ever outwork me—and that's a promise I've kept to this day. You need to start making and keeping that promise too.

15.
HOW DO YOU WANT TO BE REMEMBERED?

Living for a Bigger Purpose

I was 18 years old when I started looking at getting into real estate. The gentleman I talked to about it who was already successful in real estate started asking me questions about what I wanted to do in life.

I said, "Well, I'm in college now, so I want to play some baseball and get a degree."

I'll never forget how he looked at me and what he said: "Before you make any decision in life—especially when it comes to what you're going to do with a career—ask yourself: How do I want to be remembered?"

He was very specific. He told me to fast forward to my 82nd birthday or to my deathbed and really think about what I want my life to have looked like.

"What are three things they would say about you?" he asked.

I took a minute to think about it and said, "I want them to say I was fearless. That I was selfless. And that I was humble."

It made me think about how I wanted to find something I could do on my own to impact thousands and thousands of people. I always thought I would impact my own family, but I realized that I wanted to impact other people because when I fast-forwarded to my 82nd birthday, I got cold sweats thinking about getting to the end of my life and not impacting more.

I've watched a lot of people around me become successful, but more importantly, I've watched a lot of people become unsuccessful. I know a lot of egotistical broke people. They have no money and their egos are so big that they can't even admit it. I know they're broke, but for some reason, either they don't know it or can't accept it. I want to tell people the truth. If I'm going to be selfless and fearless, I'm not going to watch people around me lie to themselves about where they're at.

When some of the guys that I got into the insurance business with said they were doing well, and I really interrogated their reality, I found out they weren't. They were lying to themselves. And when I got through that lie, they realized how much it hurt.

You can't have a big ego and have a big business—you have to pick one. They can't go together. It's hard to have a big ego and be a good teammate. I call people out on their sh*t to help them, not hurt them. People that call you out on your sh*t to hurt you, those are bullies, or wolves. I call you out on your sh*t as a sheepdog because I want to be remembered as someone who always helped and wasn't afraid to do it.

At the end of the day, whenever you make a decision, you should always have this in the back of your mind and ingrained in you: How do you want to be remembered?

When I first launched my construction company, I was in my twenties. I said to one of the guys I was working with, "Here's what I want: No matter who I build a house for, no matter where I build it, I don't ever want to walk into a grocery store or be at a game, and see somebody and be uncomfortable because I worked on their house and something didn't go well."

I always wanted them to be able to say that I was a good dude who worked hard, was fair, and competed hard with his competition. I also didn't want to try and squeeze every dollar out of my clients. That was part of being fair.

At the end of the day, I knew unequivocally that I wanted to have an impact. I knew when I left this world and God said, "Hey, your time's up," that I didn't want to wish I had done more for people and made more of an impact. I want to give back so much that it affects people for generations. And I make every decision and live my life with that always in mind.

I hope people say I helped them out, and when they were in a bad spot, I did what I could. I want to leave a mark. I don't want to die one day and have my headstone say: "Shawn: Good bill payer." I don't want to live that way so I definitely don't want to die that way. I want to make an impact while I can.

If you want to be great at anything, you need to think with that kind of depth, always asking yourself: How do I want to be remembered? Because the alternative is what? That you were here. You made some money, but didn't share. He did what he did to be heard but not serve. Is that what you want?

So when you start thinking that way about the difference you make in the world—not just on the corner where you live or for the people you're related to—if you can live that way, everything changes. You're living for a much bigger purpose. If you're not, then you're just wasting opportunity. As long as I'm still breathing, I want to impact other people. It's what drives me on a daily basis. There are too many people out there that need help to only be thinking of yourself.

It's one of the reasons I wrote this book. I hope you're thinking, Man, that was a great book and it's going to help me out. And even if you think, Eh, I skimmed through it, didn't really like it and Shawn's an idiot, either way, I don't care because I know I set it out to write this book to help people and serve (and if you remember, you have no right to judge me anyway). Of course I want to help, but I can't live paralyzed by what you're going to say. I can give away 75% of my money and people will think that's still not enough while others will think I'm crazy for giving away that much, saying, "Who's he trying to be? Is he trying to show off?" I'm just trying to do what I think is right for me and for how I want to be remembered.

Think About the End, Live in the Now

I want people to say about me, "You know what? The dude wasn't perfect. He definitely made mistakes. But you know what?

He rebounded. When he got punched in the face from his mistakes, he got back up."

That's the fearlessness part.

"He just kept getting up. He knew people judged him and talked sh*t about him, but he didn't care. The guy just kept moving and kept getting up. He wasn't the biggest, the baddest, or the smartest, but he kept getting up."

What do you want people to say about you?

Really think about it. What will people say at your funeral if it were now? Be honest. Now, what are three things you wish they would say? You have to start thinking about those things and live that way. Think about it on a daily basis.

For example, if you want to be remembered for being humble, which is one of mine, and you think you did pretty good at something, don't next think, Hey, let me tell everyone how good I am.

If you want to make an impact and you have enough money to make a difference, you're well within your right to keep buying things, but are those kinds of decisions how you want to be remembered?

If you want to be remembered for doing what's right, and you see someone who needs someone to stand up for him, you better go help, even if it's uncomfortable, even if you'll get punched in the face.

You might be scared. It might hurt at the moment. But getting punched in the face for doing something that's right for you is always worth it.

You have to understand, these kinds of decisions are so big that they will last for generations. When I was selling life insurance, I would say, "You know, it looks like you've done pretty well by your kids and everybody around you. Do you want to be remembered as the guy where your family had to pay for your funeral because you didn't have life insurance? And that's what they'll remember about you? I mean, they'll remember the other stuff too, but the very first thing they'll remember is how you were selfish because you didn't leave your family with a policy, even though you had enough to pay for it every month."

This is the level I am talking about here. Every single decision should come back to that big question and fast forward through your life to see what it means. What does it look like and what do you have to do?

People have asked me, "Why did you decide to get sober?"

Well, I did jump off the third story of a hotel onto a freaking car in the parking lot thinking that would be faster than taking an elevator or stairs. And it took me months to heal from my cuts and breaks. But to be really honest, I wanted to have children and I never wanted them to see any of that. If I hadn't made the decision that I wanted to have children, I'm sure I wouldn't have stopped using drugs and alcohol. Or who knows, perhaps I would have ended up in jail or something. But for me, I didn't want my kids to remember me that way because I did a lot of stupid things when I was drunk.

Every decision you make will affect and alter your legacy. And when you're gone from this world, that's all you're going to have.

How will they remember you? How will they remember your impact or lack thereof on the world? That's your legacy. Legacies can be positive or negative. They're usually never in the middle. Even the good bill payer is someone who probably couldn't give back much and didn't provide much outside that, always thinking they couldn't afford it.

If nothing else comes out of this book, just don't be afraid to be punched in the face. It will then in turn make you fearless, which then in turn allows you to be more selfless, which then in turn allows you to be humble in your spirit and to be a servant. And then take that and stand up for other people through your fearlessness, and turn that into some better daily habits where you're not going to let people speak negativity into your life. That you're going to protect the way you think in order to have the mental space to have massive, audacious goals that you're probably going to miss a lot, but you're going to inspire through your large thought process. You do all that, and you're setting yourself up for some major wins.

If you can start thinking like that, you will start to see more and more opportunities and think, What else can I do? You'll start looking for opportunities to get punched in the face because you'll see that there's a massive opportunity on the other side. You won't be worried about what people think because you know you'll never go backward and you'll move forward and leave them all behind. You won't retreat, which makes you humble and fearless—and that's a good day, and you'll see every day can and will be a good day. You'll live by your north star because you know it's not talent nor brains that breed success—it's mother freaking relentlessness.

If you can do all those things, the world better watch out, because you'll be a different person. The idea that these other people that have made money are more talented is a lie and a myth and we're going to break that myth. People are going to realize that nothing should separate you from achieving the goals you want and to stop cheering so much for the bullsh*t people feed the world with their motivational speaking and their weekly or daily or quarterly life coaching they want to charge you for. The sky's the limit for you. And that's a true statement because we all can achieve together. You just need to stop being afraid of getting punched in the face to get there.

ABOUT THE AUTHOR

Shawn Meaike is the founder and president of the life insurance agency, Family First Life. In late 2013, Shawn launched FFL, currently on track to be a billion-dollar independent marketing organization just nine short years later. As Shawn describes it, he has "built a company that truly puts both the families of our clients and the families of our agents first." Family First Life is now represented by over 20,000 licensed agents in all 50 states marketing mortgage protection, final expense, life insurance, and annuities.

Shawn started his independence at a young age. He didn't come from money and was raised by a single mother who taught him that work ethic is the key to survival. Using sports as an outlet from his troubled environment, Shawn attended junior college to play baseball. After realizing he wouldn't get paid to play, he saved up and transferred to Eastern Connecticut State University to focus on working and going to school full time. With a voracious hunger to serve others, this is where he fell in love with social work. After graduating, he went on to work as a Child Protective Services Investigator for the State of Connecticut for 13 years.

After many figurative *punches in the face*, Shawn decided to get sober at the age of 28. This is where the hustle and grit he exhibits today was born. In 2008 he left his full-time job at the state to further his position in helping people, while simultaneously finding a way for him, and the people around him to get wealthy. As a father of two, it was a tough decision, but he knew it was the necessary step to take to provide a life for his family that he did not have himself.

From 2008 to 2013, Shawn ran various businesses including but not limited to residential and commercial real estate sales, land development, general contracting, owed property as a landlord, and ran a waste management company, but found his niche as an independent life insurance agent for another company before starting his own. He knew the company he was working for didn't provide the necessary opportunities for his success, so he took that leap of faith and built his own company from the ground up. Shawn has given more than he can put into words to build FFL, thousands of dollars in debt, maxed out credit cards, and countless sleepless nights for the singular purpose of building something larger than himself.

This man simply never takes his foot off the gas, which is why he has been able to accomplish so much in life and in business. In all his success, what gives Shawn the greatest sense of fulfillment is being able to give away money to countless organizations including but not limited to Make-A-Wish Foundation, Children Hospitals across the U.S. and Puerto Rico, and the Dream Center Foundation, where 50% of this book's proceeds are pledged to.

Shawn does not consider himself a rare breed or special. He's simply a firm believer that with the right attitude and activity, anything is possible.